ONE DEEP BREATH
A NOVEL OF TRUTH AND KNOWING
Evie's Resolution

....

VICTORIA WRIGHT

© Copyright 2022 by Victoria Wright All rights reserved.
No part of this book may be reproduced in any form without permission in writing from the author. Reviewers may quote brief passages in review.
Published March 2022

DISCLAIMER

No part of this publication may be reproduced or transmitted in any form or by any means, mechanical or electronic, including photocopying or recording, or by any information storage and retrieval system, or transmitted by email without permission in writing from the author. Neither the author nor the publisher assumes any responsibility for errors, omissions, or contrary interpretations of the subject matter herein. The characters in this book are entirely fictional. Any resemblance to actual persons living or dead is entirely coincidental. Any perceived slight of any individual or organization is purely unintentional.

Table of Contents

CHAPTER 1 — LEAP OF FAITH 1

CHAPTER 2 — CONGRATULATIONS 5

CHAPTER 3 — SMOKE 16

CHAPTER 4 — PAYING IT FORWARD 29

CHAPTER 5 — WHAT FRIENDS DO 41

CHAPTER 6 — BIG GIRL PANTS 56

CHAPTER 7 — MAGIC IN A CUP 65

CHAPTER 8 — SPECIAL FRIEND 73

CHAPTER 9 — STORIES 86

CHAPTER 10 — TRUST THE PROCESS 100

CHAPTER 11 — TWO PEAS IN A POD 109

CHAPTER 12 — SUNSHINE STUDIO 122

CHAPTER 13 — CARED FOR 132

CHAPTER 14 — HOME 148

CHAPTER 15 — THIS AWAITS YOU 156

CHAPTER 16 — ALWAYS WITH YOU 165

REFERENCES 172

ABOUT THE AUTHOR 175

CHAPTER 1 — LEAP OF FAITH

It seemed liked forever before I could say a word as thoughts raced through my mind. I loved him, but what about my new life on Martha's Vineyard? What about Aja? Could he leave her, or did he have to stay in Colorado? I wiped the tears from my eyes.

Hendrix gazed down at me, his eyes filled with love. Not expecting me to hesitate before answering his marriage proposal, his face then turned from love to concern.

"Evie, are you okay? Is there something wrong?"

"I didn't think I would ever hear those words said to me. I want to say yes, but ..."

"But, what?"

I lowered my head. "I am scared."

"Scared of what?"

"Hendrix, I love you, but can this work? Now that Aja is in your life, you need to be with her. She is so young and needs a full-time father. I enjoy my new life on the island and being near my granddad. I don't want to move back to Colorado. How can this possibly work?" I asked, my eyes still filled with tears.

"Evie, slow down and breathe." He watched me take a few deep breaths. "Do you want to spend your life with me?"

"Of course."

"Well, then we will figure this out."

"But, how?" I asked, my voice filled with trepidation.

"Do you believe we can create the life we desire?"

"Yes, you know I do."

"Then we will create the life we desire." Hendrix took my hand in his. "Evie Prince, will you marry me?"

I looked deep into his soulful eyes and took a deep breath. "Hendrix Talisman, yes, I will marry you."

***

It felt like I was floating the entire hike back to the car. Our smiles and the love that we felt for each other created an energy that even strangers could feel. We then had an intimate dinner at a fantastic little noodle shop to celebrate. I smiled so much my face hurt.

That night, as we lay in bed, I turned to Hendrix. "We can figure this out, right?"

"Evie, please do not worry. We will make this work. Stay open to all the possibilities." From under his pillow, he pulled out a simple yet stunning emerald ring, flanked by a diamond on each side, and slipped it on my finger. "Evie, this ring represents the love that I share with you."

The brilliance of the ring took my breath away. "This is absolutely beautiful."

"To me, you symbolize the emerald. The stone of successful love, it opens the heart and nurtures the heart chakra. It embodies compassion, unity, and unconditional love. That is what you and your energy give to me." He then kissed me, and we fell into oneness.

***

The week had come to an end. At the airport, my heart was heavy leaving Hendrix, but we were committed to each other and, in time, we would live our lives together.

As the plane climbed higher in the sky, I looked at the Denver landscape. So much had changed, including me, but could I live here again? The thought was too much for me to handle. I looked at my ring, smiled, then closed my eyes and fell asleep.

When Granddad picked me up at the boat, I felt like a walking zombie. Going to a destination always seemed easier than coming back.

Granddad welcomed me with an enormous hug. "Hey, kid, how was your trip?"

"Amazing."

"I can tell you're tired, but I can see a sparkle in your eyes. Everything work out with you two?"

I held up my left hand and smiled.

"Whoa. Seems like it worked out better than expected." He chuckled. "Congratulations."

"Thank you."

We walked to Granddad's truck, and I put my bag in the back.

The drive up island gave me peace. I glanced over at Granddad and could tell he was thinking.

"So, is this something that will happen soon, or …?"

"No, we still have things to work out, but we know we want to spend our lives together. We just have to figure out how we can do it."

"Is he willing to move here?"

"Before finding out about his daughter, I would have said yes. But now, who knows? Aja is only three years old, and she needs him, and I know he cannot live without her. So, there lies the dilemma."

We were both silent until we pulled onto my road. That was when Granddad hesitantly asked, "Would you move back to Colorado?"

"I don't know. My life here on the island and being with you has been amazing. I can't imagine not being here."

"Well, just stay open, and I am sure you both will create the life that you want to live together."

I smiled. "That is exactly what Hendrix said."

CHAPTER 2 — CONGRATULATIONS

Sleeping in my own bed felt good, but I missed waking up next to Hendrix. On my bedside table was the sweet picture of him and Aja. Seeing their faces put me in a wonderful mood, even though I was still sluggish because of the two-hour time difference between here and Denver.

I grabbed my phone and texted Hendrix. *I love you*, was all I said.

Walking through the house, I opened the door to the extra bedroom and was greeted by my paintings. Something new appeared every time I looked at them. I felt the emotions and looked forward to what I would paint next.

Before breakfast, I walked out on the deck to breathe in the moist air. The salty air filled my lungs and, as I exhaled, a sense of calm came over me. I sat on the deck, leaned up against the house, and entered my meditation.

"Thank you for helping me to create this wonderful life."

"*You focused and manifested your desires.*"

"How will Hendrix and I live our lives together?"

"*Patience and focus. The power of two will bring you what you both desire.*"

I sat in silence for a few more minutes, soaking up the tranquility, and then I heard Granddad next door.

"Good morning!" I yelled over.

"Hey, sleepyhead, I didn't think you would ever wake up."

"It's only eight o'clock," I whined.

"Need some coffee?"

"Please."

"Come on; I'll make you breakfast."

"Be right over." Spending time with Granddad gave me pure joy. The thought of not having him near me almost brought me to tears. I needed to savor every moment I had with him.

"So, have you told your BFF, Reva, yet about your engagement?"

"BFF?" I laughed.

"Never too old to learn new things, right?"

"Right. And no, I haven't told her yet, but I plan to call her today."

Granddad handed me a plate of scrambled eggs, potatoes, and bacon.

"Mmm … This is so good. Thank you," I told him after taking a delicious bite.

"Breakfast is the most important meal of the day."

I nodded absentmindedly then asked, "So, Granddad, I know word will get around town about my engagement, but should I say something to Steve?"

"There is no need. He will hear. He may feel a bit embarrassed and act standoffish. In time, he will come back around, and you will be friends just like before."

"I hope so. He is a wonderful person. I don't want to lose his friendship."

"So, what is on your agenda today?"

"Unpack, laundry, and I was also hoping to paint."

"I need to go over to the tribal office. Wanted to know if you would like to come with."

"Sure, I've never been there."

"I'll yell over in an hour. Need to do a few more things before we head out."

I thanked Granddad for the excellent breakfast then slipped back through the bushes. By the time I had unpacked and started a load of laundry, Granddad was ready to go.

"Hey, kid, ready?"

"Yup, be right over."

***

The tribal office was just a few miles down the main road. A large rock at the entryway marked the turnoff. I had always wondered what was down that road. Off to the right of the entrance was a housing development, and then there was the tribal building.

As we entered the lobby, I saw portraits hanging all over the walls. I studied each one then noticed Granddad's photo.

"When did you do this?" I asked.

"Oh, that. A few years back. When you become an elder, they take your picture and hang it up. I'm an elder a few times over, but I had never let them take my picture. Finally, someone came down to the boat and snapped that shot."

"Wait—so who are all these people?"

"They are all tribal members. Your relatives."

"Really?"

From down the hall, we heard, "Hey, Attaquin, long time no see!" Then a man in his late sixties with his grey tied back hair and the same sun-worn complexion as Granddad walked toward us.

"Hey, Louie, how have you been?" Granddad and Louie shook hands.

"Great. Where have you been keeping yourself?"

"Just fishing and keeping an eye on my granddaughter."

Louie looked over at me. "Granddaughter?"

"Yup, Louie meet Evie. This is Paul's daughter."

Louie offered his hand and gave me a vigorous handshake. "Evie, so nice to meet you." He then looked me up and down. "Yup, I can see Paul in you. So, where have you been hiding?"

"Hiding?" I asked.

"She was living out in Colorado. Just moved back a year ago," Granddad explained.

"Well, welcome home. Always good to be with family."

"Thank you. And yes, I agree it is great to be with family."

I continued walking around and noticed another picture. The man looked a lot like Granddad.

"Who is this?"

"That's my brother, and over there is my sister."

A tall, heavy-set woman with thick, wavy brown hair and long, beaded earrings walked over to us. "Attaquin, are you ready?"

"Yes. Evie, wait out here. I won't be too long." The two entered a nearby office and shut the door.

"Do you know who that is?" Louie asked. I had felt him watching me as I looked at the pictures.

"No, I don't know any of these people, other than Granddad."

"Well, that is Dorothy. She was my aunt, and since Attaquin and I are cousins, she would be your great-great-aunt."

"Hmm ... I never knew I had so much family. I knew little about my mother's extended family and, as you may have figured, I am just learning about my father's side of the family."

"Any time you want to know more, just let me know. I like to think I am an unofficial historian for the tribe."

"That is wonderful to know. I am sure I will take you up on that offer."

"Nice meeting you, Evie, and welcome home."

I strolled around some more, looking at all the portraits. Each one told a different story. Some of the people were seated and dressed in their best; others were captured in everyday street clothes. The photos that I loved to look at the most were the ones in their traditional regalia—the details, beading, and wampum. No matter what they wore, I could feel their presence, all of whom demanded respect.

Down the hall, I noticed a great room. A fireplace made out of natural stones filled one wall. The other had huge windows that looked out onto a beautiful pasture. The scenery was incredible.

I exited through a single door that led out to a deck and soaked in the beauty. Immediately, an energy of peace and comfort ran throughout my body, something that I had never felt before. It felt like I was home.

I heard Granddad calling me and returned to the lobby.

"All done," he said.

"All done with what?" I asked.

"Your paperwork for membership."

"What membership?"

"Membership into the tribe."

I gave Granddad a blank look. "I'm sorry, Granddad, but I'm not following."

"Let's go out to the deck, and I will explain."

There were two seats over in the corner of the deck that gave us some privacy.

Granddad slowly lowered himself into the chair, took a deep breath, and then smiled at me. "Evie, our people have been on this island for over ten thousand years. We were the first inhabitants of this land and survived the unspeakable atrocities that were levied against our people. In 1987, the federal government acknowledged our existence, and they federally recognized us as a tribe. We were not alone, as our sister tribes' homelands are on the Cape."

"But, if we have been around for thousands of years, what took them so long?"

Granddad laughed. "That's a discussion for another day. To gain membership, you have to prove your lineage. This is something that your father and I had wanted to do for you since you were born. But, if we did so, then you would have known who your father was, and that was not what he wanted. It may have taken a few years—forty plus—but once they have approved the paperwork, you can legally be a member of the tribe."

"Wow, this is a lot to take in. I don't know how to feel about this. It is comforting to know that I am a part of something, but …"

"You only knew half your story. We never wanted to deny you the right to know about your indigenous culture. I hope this is something that you would like to learn more about." Granddad paused then took my hand. "Evie, this is a part of who you are."

We sat in silence, and I closed my eyes. The peaceful energy that I had felt earlier returned.

Granddad looked over at me and noticed the smile on my face. "Whatcha thinking, kid?"

"There has always been something that I felt was different about me. Not only was my skin darker than my mother's, but I didn't always feel that I belonged. Most of the time, I thought it was because I didn't have a father, but now, being here, I realize it was more than that. Being with you and learning about my indigenous side, I feel like I have found home. Thank you."

***

When we got back to the house, I headed straight for the studio. My goal was to capture the energy that I had felt at the tribal office—the feeling of comfort and peace.

Spring had not yet sprung, so the colors that I witnessed today were muted yet mesmerizing. Greens, browns, blues, light yellow, grey. Everything felt washed out, like the ocean wind had blown the color away. Still, it felt warm and inviting to me. After a few hours, I had the beginnings of an abstract landscape. Then I went into the house to make a cup of tea and check my phone. Hendrix had called.

"Sorry I missed your call. How are you?"

"I am amazing."

"Really?"

"Yes, because I have a wonderful woman who wants to spend her life with me."

Goosebumps ran up my arms. "Funny you should say that. I have the most amazing man who wants to spend his life with me."

"Huh. Well, I guess we are two blessed people."

"Yes, we are."

"So, what have you been up to today?"

"Granddad and I had an incredible morning." I explained the tribal membership process and learning more about my indigenous side.

"Wow, that is wonderful. How do you feel?"

"I feel like I am home. There is just a peace here that I have never felt before."

"Will you take me over there when I come out?"

"Of course. Are you coming soon?"

"I would like to make a trip out there by the end of the month, if you will have me."

"I may not let you leave," I teased. "How is Aja doing?"

"She is a happy little girl. I told her about me proposing to you. She approved."

"Aw … That is so sweet."

"Evie, there is a lot that we need to discuss, and I would prefer that we do that in person."

"I agree. In my meditation, I asked how we can make this work, and I was told patience and focus. The power of two will bring what we desire."

"I heard something similar. Evie, this will work. We have the power to create. Hey, I gotta run. Will call you later. Love ya."

"Love you!"

I relaxed and enjoyed my tea for a few moments then called Reva.

"Hey, girl, what's up?"

"Have a moment?"

"Sure, I am between meetings. Everything okay?"

"Better than okay. Hendrix and I are engaged!" I squealed out.

"What? Congratulations. How do you feel?"

"Amazing."

"I am so happy for you. So, I guess I really need to meet this man."

"Yes, you do."

"Have you set a date yet?"

"No, there are still many things that we have to figure out, but we are in no rush. Patience and focus."

"That is exactly the right mindset. As you well know, Brian and I are still combining our lives. I think the longer you have been single, the more difficult it can be. There are just certain non-negotiables." Excitedly, Reva then said, "So, let me see the ring."

I took a picture of my paint-splattered hand with my stunning emerald ring and sent it to her.

"Ooo ... Girl, that ring is gorgeous."

"Thank you."

"Shoot, shoot, shoot. I have a call on the other line. I gotta go. Congratulations, and I love ya."

"Love you, too."

I looked at my ring and could feel the moment that Hendrix had slipped it on my finger all over again. *We will make this work. I know we will.*

***

As I was straightening up the house, I realized I hadn't returned the Sci-Fi movies from before I had left for Denver. Four o'clock. The library was still open, so I jumped in the car and headed over.

It was a quiet afternoon at the library, which was completely different than during the summer. Just a few cars parked outside. When I opened the door, the warmth from the heater gave me an instant cozy feeling.

"Hey, Barbra, how are you doing?"

"Evie, haven't seen you in a little while. Where have you been?"

I slid the movies across the counter. "Oh, I just got back from a trip to Colorado."

The sparkle of my ring caught Barbra's eye. "Ooo ... I see you have a new ring. Anything you would like to share?" she asked coyly.

I looked around to see if there was anyone else in the library. There was a couple in the back, but I didn't see anyone else. I turned back to Barbra. "Actually, I just got engaged!" I half-whispered and half-shrieked.

"Wow-wee! Congratulations. Anyone I know?"

"No, he's back in Colorado."

"So, is he moving out here, or are you going back?"

"That is something that we are still working out."

"Well, I am happy for you."

"Thank you. Hey, do you have any new Sci-Fi movies?"

"Yup, a few were just returned. I already put them up on the shelf."

I walked around the corner to the movie section and realized that Steve had been there the whole time and had overheard my news. When our eyes met, my face flushed. He looked away then said, "Congratulations on your engagement. He is a lucky guy."

"Thank you. I appreciate that."

He turned and quickly left the library.

When I went to the desk to check out the new movies, Barbra gave me a *whoops* look but said nothing further.

Driving home, my emotions were up and down. Was Steve mad or embarrassed? Should I have told him when we had first met that I was in a relationship? But I hadn't been back then, not really. Well, I kind of sort of was, but it had been on pause. Plus, how was I supposed to know that he would like me? *Ugh!*

CHAPTER 3 — SMOKE

Life as a single woman hadn't always been easy. Sure, I enjoyed the freedom, but there were many days when I would dream about finding a partner and having a family. However, there was always something else that I could not put my finger on that called to me. Even before starting this journey of finding my happiness and true self, I'd had a longing to see new and different things. Changing jobs and moving to a new city had never really bothered me, as I enjoyed being in new places. Maybe because I had been running from myself and it had given me a new opportunity to not think about it, or maybe because it was something else. I wondered if my grandfather was right and I had their free spirit. Now that I knew more about my family I could better understand how they had felt. I just didn't know if my desire to see the world would allow me to leave my family to do it.

Lately, it had been crossing my mind what my life would have been like if I could have embraced that free spirit that my grandfather had so purposefully quashed. Where would I be and what type of person would I have become? *Hmph*, I would never know, so no more what-ifs.

The person I had become resulted from the circumstances of my upbringing, but I no longer had to live as others thought I should. I had the choice to create a new and different life, the ability to create *my* perfect life.

Staring out the window, I wondered, *What is my perfect life?*

Not that long ago, I would have had an answer instantaneously—money, security, success, house, cars, etcetera, etcetera. But now new desires were emerging. My perfect life was filled with creativity, family, beauty, health, travel, food, experiences, spirituality, peace, love, and joy. Oh, and I couldn't forget financial security. I possessed many of those things already, but if I were truly honest with myself, I desired to have them all. Was that selfish? Some might say so, but if I didn't desire and create it, then who would? Why did it have to be this or that? Why couldn't it be this *and* that? Why should I have to sacrifice my desires for someone else's? Was that my duty as a wife, girlfriend, friend, or mother, or was it their duty to find their own happiness and to create the life that they desired?

At that moment, it seemed like I was looking at the world through my grandfather's and mother's eyes. I realized how they had been able to do what made them happy. They had not left their family to do humanitarian work; they had created a life that allowed them to do what they loved and still be with those who they loved. My grandmother had known what my grandfather had to do to be happy, and she had supported him. Just like they had done for my mother. Each and every one of us had the choice to discover what made us happy and to then create a life filled with that happiness. I had thought my family was selfish for doing what they had done but, in hindsight, they had been teaching me one of the greatest lessons—you truly could have it all; you just had to create it.

***

The ping from an incoming text made me look over at my phone.

Evie, I have the most amazing news. Call when you can. Tatum, flashed across the screen.

I put my brush down and gave her a call.

"Evie, I have the best news."

"What's up? You sound so excited."

"Well, the interview with the Bali tourism magazine is a go. The newest hotel in Bali has received a lot of attention, but the piece that the hotel owner, Mr. Pratama, commissioned from you has brought even more interest. They would like to interview you both."

"That is fantastic news!"

"Do you have a professional headshot? You will need one for the article. The magazine is sending over the questions, and we will set the interview call for next Thursday. Bali is twelve hours ahead of you and fourteen hours ahead of me, so we still need to pick a time that works for all. Once I receive the questions, I will send them right over, and let me know if you would like to discuss your answers beforehand."

All of this was overwhelming me. I could feel my anxiety increasing. Why did people want to know about me? I got really uncomfortable talking about myself.

"Evie, are you still there?"

"Yes, I am here."

"You okay? Isn't this great?"

"Yes, it's amazing, but I am not great at talking about myself. You don't want to know how long it took me to write my bio on my website."

Tatum laughed. "This is something that you will need to get used to. Your commission piece was like a coming-out party. Now people want to know more about you. Mr. Pratama is very supportive of the people who work with and for him. If he likes you, it goes a long way. He has hotels across Indonesia, so there could be more opportunity for you to work with him. The more press you get, the more press he gets," she explained.

"Okay, I get it. Putting my big girl pants on. I can do this."

"Yes, you can. Watch your email."

"Will do. Thanks, Tatum."

"This is all you. I'm just the facilitator."

After we ended the call, my mind raced, making it impossible for me to continue painting, so I cleaned up and called it a day.

Professional headshot. I wonder who I can get to do that, I thought to myself.

Beth. She had probably had one done for her website, so I called her.

"Hey, Evie."

"Hi, Beth, how are you?"

"Well. I guess congratulations are in order."

"Congratulations? Oh, you heard?"

"You know news like that travels fast around here. Will you get married here or back in Colorado?"

"Actually, we haven't gotten that far. Still a few kinks to work out."

"Gotcha. What can I do for you?"

"I need a professional headshot for a magazine interview, but all I have are cell phone selfies."

"Congratulations! Things are moving quickly for you," she praised. "Well, actually, my cousin, Steve, took my headshot."

"Oh, I see," I said under my breath. "He is a man of many talents. Builder, web designer, and now photographer. Might you know of anyone else?"

"Why, I am sure he would love to do a photo session with you. Wait—is there something going on between you two?"

I gave a momentary pause. "Let's just say he was very surprised I got engaged."

"Ah-ha. I see. Let me think. There are a couple of local people I know. I'll text you their contact information."

"Nice! Beth, I don't know what I would do without you. You have been instrumental in the progression of my painting career here on the island. Your generosity and openness mean the world to me. Thank you. I really appreciate you."

"As I said before, I believe in raising all ships. There is always more room for artists on this island. The world could use more beauty in it, and if I can help those who create beauty, we will all benefit."

***

My day started off well. A good night's sleep, substantial breakfast, and then I picked up my phone to read the news. I rarely read the news, but it was like I wanted to go deeper into the rat hole of negativity.

Every article I read was worse than the last, making me sit there in a puddle of gloom. The world was a mess. So much was wrong. How could anyone find peace?

A heavy feeling consumed me. It felt like I had the weight of the world on me. How could I have it all and create my perfect life when so many had nothing?

When I stopped and focused, I realized there was a soundtrack of negative thoughts running through my head about things that I had no control over. Where had this come from?

Then I smelled something ... *Cigarette smoke? Who the hell is smoking?*

I went to the window to see if someone had walked up the road. No one. Then I walked around outside. Back in the house, I checked every room, trying to find the source. *How can I possibly smell cigarette smoke when there is no one here but me?* The smell put me in an even worse mood because I despised cigarettes.

In an attempt to clear my nose, I opened the door and windows, but the smell was still there. It drove me crazy! I threw up an S.O.S. to Hendrix via text.

I seriously think I am going crazy. Please call.

Not more than ten minutes later, the phone rang.

In a strained voice, I heard, "Evie, what's wrong?"

"I really think I am going crazy. I keep on smelling cigarette smoke, and there is no one here but me. It's so strong that it's like I am the one smoking."

There was a long pause, and then Hendrix released a loud exhale. "Oh, Evie, you are not going crazy, but you have something on your mind. What has been going on?"

"I don't know. The day started off great, but then something set me off, and I found myself angry and negative. Reading the news only made my mood worse. This world is a mess. I just feel so frustrated and angry."

"Well, there is plenty in this world to be upset about, but it sounds like there is something deeper that is putting you in this state. Your higher self is giving you a nudge to quiet your mind and focus on what is troubling you."

"Isn't it odd that I would smell cigarettes?"

"Do you like the smell?"

"No, I hate that smell."

"Well, that is why you are smelling it. Whatever this worry is, it has been with you for a while. You are being asked to finally focus on it."

"How on earth would you know that?"

"It happened to me before, but mine was a constant taste of garlic. I love garlic, but I hate the lingering aftertaste when I eat too much. My spiritual response resulted from seeing my father at a family event. He acted like I was his long-lost son. Memories of his physical and verbal abuse came flooding back and haunted me until I could process and release my anger. Only then did the horrible taste go away. So, there is something that has triggered that smell for you. Until you deal with it will the smell go away."

"Well, my higher self is pushing hard because the smell is debilitating."

"Evie, be kind to yourself. It may take time to manage this."

"Thank you, Hendrix. What would I do without you?"

"Live your life, but I am glad that you have chosen me to live it with you."

"I have. Every time I look at my ring, I get goosebumps." I heard Aja laughing in the background. "I'm sorry. I didn't know Aja was with you."

"Don't worry; she is spending the afternoon with me. Her mother had an appointment."

"How are things between you two?"

"We have our ups and downs. Her mother has been having a few health issues. She assures me that she's okay, but our relationship is definitely impacted when she is not feeling well."

"Is it serious?"

"I believe it is more serious than she is leading me to believe. But I need to trust that she will keep me posted on how she is doing."

"Does Aja know there's something up?"

"Sort of. She tells me when her mother isn't feeling well, but she says it so matter-of-factly, like she's used to it. Hard to believe she can manage this at such a young age."

Hendrix hesitated. "Evie, you need to release the negativity you are feeling and change your perspective on how you are viewing the issue that is worrying you. Worry comes from the unknown of what may happen in the future, which means you are not living in the present. You cannot control the future, but you can control how you manage the present. Take your time and think long and hard about what is troubling you. When you identify it, ask your higher self if this is the issue that you need to focus on. You will receive your answer."

After Hendrix finished, I gave myself a moment to think.

"Beautiful, you okay?"

"Yes, I wonder what the issue could be."

"Ask your higher self for clarity. It may be a repressed emotion."

"Okay, I will do that. I don't want to take you away from Aja any longer. Call me tonight if you can. I love you."

"I love you, too, Evie."

***

The cigarette smell was so constant and strong that it triggered a thumping headache. If I wasn't careful, it would turn into a full-blown migraine. I rushed into the bathroom to grab some headache medicine. My hands were unsteady, and I dropped the bottle into the sink, losing half the pills down the drain. Shakely, I grabbed the remaining pills and stuffed them back into the bottle. The smell was becoming unbearable.

I lifted my head to see my reflection in the mirror. *Ugh*, I looked like shit. What was going on with me?

I took two pills and popped them into my mouth. Then I heard, "*Spit them out.*"

"Huh? You want me to spit these out?"

"*You do not need them. Listen to your heart.*"

In a pained whine, I asked, "Are you kidding me?" I hung my head, debating what to do, then I spat the pills into the sink. "Happy now?" I groaned.

"*Meditate and listen to your heart.*"

My head was thumping so strongly that my body crumpled in on itself. I couldn't stand up straight, and the light coming into the room aggravated my headache even more.

Moving gingerly, so as not to move my head too much, I drew my bedroom curtains and crawled into the bed. I lay down carefully, closed my eyes, and took one deep breath to ground myself. I continued to breathe deeply until the thumping softened.

"*Evie, what is on your mind?*"

"There has been a lot on my mind. The magazine interview, Granddad's health, my desire to travel, how Hendrix and I are going ..." I stopped mid-sentence. Immediately, a sense of clarity came over me. I was worried about how Hendrix and I were going to live our lives together. "That's it."

"*Do you trust I will always guide and care for you?*"

"Yes."

"*Then declare it, and it will be so.*"

The next thing I knew, it was two hours later, and I woke to a clear head. Only a faint smell of cigarettes lingered.

Now that I know what the issue is, how do I stop worrying about it? I wondered.

It was still early enough to pop over and see Granddad. Maybe he could help me figure this out.

After slipping through the bushes, I heard him out back, in the shed.

"Granddad, what are you doing? It's late."

"Oh, I was looking for something."

"Can I help you?"

"No, I will look again tomorrow. What's up? How was your day?"

"Well, I've had better."

"What's wrong?"

I began by telling him my revelation about my mother and grandfather. Then I told him about smelling cigarette smoke, and lastly that I had identified the worry that caused the smoke smell.

"Geez, that is a lot of thinking, kid. Let's go inside, and I'll make us something hot to drink so we can talk about it."

Following behind Granddad, I noticed he was walking a little slower than normal. When we got inside, I offered to heat the water while he sat down.

"How are you feeling today, Granddad?"

"Never better."

"Good. Do we need to refill your prescription yet?"

"Nope, I should have another week left."

"When is your next check-in with the doctor?"

"Evie, why are you so interested in my health?"

"I am always interested. Just want to make sure that you stay around for a long, long time."

He smiled. "So, smelling cigarette smoke, huh?"

"Yes, and I hate it. I need to figure out how to stop it." The kettle whistled, and I made us two cups of tea. I placed a steaming mug in front of Granddad.

"Thanks, kid. First, you will need to change your perspective on the smoke smell."

"Change my perspective? What do you mean?"

"Even though the smoke smell annoys you, embrace it and view it as a signal or reminder. Every emotion, ache, or pain that you feel is an indicator of what is going on inside of you. Seems like smoke is an indicator that you are worrying. Don't fight it. Appreciate the signal and ask for guidance on how to overcome the worry."

"Wow, appreciate the smell of cigarette smoke? I don't know if I can do that."

"Evie, you can do anything that you focus on."

I stared into my mug, contemplating what Granddad had just said. "Okay, I hear what you are saying, but how do I stop worrying?"

"Let me ask you this: what is the worst that can happen between you and Hendrix?"

"That's easy. We won't live our lives together."

"Now."

"Huh? What do you mean?"

"Evie, I don't know what is going to happen, but I believe that you can create the life that you desire. That life, however, may not be within the timeframe that you think it should be. Maybe it is not time for you and Hendrix to be together. The Universe may have other plans."

"But I have waited so long to love someone."

"I know, kid, but it has also been a long time coming for you to love yourself." Granddad could see that I was becoming upset. "Evie, would you worry so much if you knew in your soul that you and Hendrix would be together, but it would still take time for it to happen?"

I sat there for a few moments, pondering the question. "Probably not. Actually, in a weird way, it would be a relief, because I could have the freedom to discover more of myself. But I would miss Hendrix."

"Is it an all or nothing? Seems like he is pretty busy with Aja."

"True, but I would want to share my experiences with him."

"And you have to be married to do that?"

I hesitated. "No."

"Give yourself some grace and know that Spirit has a plan, and you may not understand what it is, but in the end, you will receive what you desire and more."

After a moment, I pushed back my chair and got up. I brought my mug to the sink then turned toward Granddad. With a smile, I told him, "Thank you. You always know what I need. You better not get old on me."

"*Ha*. Trying not to, kid, trying not to."

Before leaving, I gave Granddad an enormous hug. "See you tomorrow."

"Not if I see you first."

***

To work through my feelings, I went to the studio to paint. Ironically, my inspiration was smoke. I needed to appreciate this guidance, and the only way that I knew I could get to that point was to paint it out.

The swirling dance of smoke that rose from a burning cigarette. Puffs of smoke as they were blown in the air from an exhale. The wrinkles that form when the smoker purses their lips. Then the gratification as the smoke seeped into the lungs. Fiery orange to signify the cigarette embers, white to represent the swirling smoke, grey for the cloudiness that it created within me. How I hated the smell of cigarette smoke, but I knew this was a reminder that ego was alive and well within me and that I was limiting myself through worry.

I closed my eyes and took a deep breath. My nose filled with the smell, and I allowed it to sit with me. Ultimately, I envisioned my worry rolled up into a cigarette. Striking the match, I was ready to let the worry go. Each inhale burned more of the worry, then the release through each exhale. Finally, the smoke would dissipate and clarity would appear. When I walked out of the studio, I had a new appreciation for the reminder that I had been given. If I fed into the worry, it would grow. But, if I recognized it for what it was and let my heart take over, the smell would float away, just like my worry.

CHAPTER 4 — PAYING IT FORWARD

My phone rang. Not recognizing the number and wanting to dissuade any telemarketers, I put on my mean voice. "Hello?"

"Yes, I am looking for Ms. Prince."

"This is she. May I ask who is calling?"

"Hi, my name is Susan Patrick, and I am the principal at the high school. I am calling to inform you that we have approved your program."

"I'm sorry? My program?"

"Yes, the program that you and the late Bill Frank proposed to the school board has been approved."

My silence showed the need for further explanation.

"The painting program to help our students manage their emotions. Bill submitted a complete proposal."

"Wow, he did it."

"I'm sorry. What did you say?"

"I didn't realize that Mr. Frank had done that. We discussed it when I was teaching at the school, but he unfortunately wasn't able to tell me that he had developed the program. May I see the plan?"

Her voice softened. "Of course. Well, I hope this is something that you still want to pursue. We feel just as strongly as Bill did that this is a much-needed program. He said that, if he had a program like this when he was in school, he would have been able to process his emotions and ultimately would have made better decisions in his life. He spoke highly of you as the architect and the head of the program."

"Thank you. Yes, can you give me some time to review everything, and I will get right back to you?"

"Sure, I will send the plan over immediately. Ms. Prince, I am sorry to surprise you with this information. I was sure that Bill had informed you, but his untimely death shocked us all."

"No worries. I just need some time to get my head around all of this."

"I understand. Thank you, and have a good evening."

I had almost forgotten about the program. Mr. Frank had said nothing to me about it since our initial discussion. However, I remembered him proclaiming that, if he got this approved, it would be the Evie show.

A *ding* from my phone snapped me out of my deep thoughts. The email from Principal Patrick contained the proposal and her contact information.

Before I opened the email, I took a deep breath and let my thoughts drift to the wonderful times that Mr. Frank and I had had together. He had truly been my only friend at the high school when I had arrived on the island to live with my grandparents after my mother had died. He would always know the right thing to say and let me know I wasn't alone. Then, as an adult, he had just seemed to know what was good for me. He must have been channeling my father. He had been a man who lived up to his promises, and the promise he had made to my father to look out for me had been no exception.

Remembering all those special moments raised my energy. I was open and ready to read the proposal that Mr. Frank had submitted.

Right in front of me, at the top of the page, was the program title. I laughed as soon as I saw it.

The Something-Something Painting Program
Submitted by Bill Frank and Evie Prince.

The long and the short of the plan was that it would be a drop-in program a few times a week after school. Students, through their guidance counselor, could opt into the program. Counselors could also recommend that a student attend. It was a time for these students to learn how to paint, have a dialogue with a counselor or each other, and to use painting as a tool to express their feelings. Mr. Frank had proposed I would lead the painting component, and he would lead the counseling sessions. However, without Mr. Frank, I didn't know how I would move forward.

As I sat there, mulling over the situation, I closed my eyes and felt a tingling at the top of my head. Then I heard, *"Ask him."* When I opened my eyes, I knew what I had to do, but would he do it?

I picked up my phone, searched through my contacts, then called.

"Hello, this is Steve. Sorry I missed your call. Please leave me a message."

"Hi, Steve, this is Evie. I hope you have been well. It seems like I haven't seen you much lately. I hoped I could grab some of your time to discuss a proposal that Mr. Frank and I had talked about prior to his death. Please let me know if you are available. Thank you." After I hung up, I sent positive thoughts his way, hoping he would return my call.

Granddad had been gone all day, so I slipped through the bushes to see him and tell him about this new opportunity.

"Come on in."

"Hey, Granddad. Haven't seen you all day. Wanted to check in and see how you were doing."

"Hi, kid. All is good. Been visiting with Steve."

"Steve? I just called him."

"Really?"

"Yes. Another reason I came over was to tell you about a program that Mr. Frank and I had discussed prior to his death to do at the high school. Little did I know, but Mr. Frank drew up a proposal and the school board approved it. The principal just called me today to tell me the good news."

"Wow, Evie, that is great."

"It is, but it was supposed to be Mr. Frank and I doing this together. He was supposed to do the counseling, and I would teach them how they could use their emotions in their paintings. Steve came to mind as the person who could do the counseling since painting has been helping him manage his addiction and emotions."

"You are right; he would be great."

"Do you think he would do it?"

"That's a good question. He is working through some things right now, so I don't know. All you can do is hold space for him as he manages his issues and know that you will find a replacement for Mr. Frank."

"I asked the principal to give me some time to review so, hopefully, Steve will respond soon. I really think this program will help a lot of students, but I can't do it alone."

"Don't worry, Evie; just know it will work out fine. Remember, you have the ability to create."

I gave Granddad a smile. "Yes, thanks for the reminder. I need to stay positive."

***

Over the next week, during my meditations, I focused on the Something-Something Painting Program and knew that all would work out just as it should.

"Granddad, I am heading to the dump. Do you need me to take anything?"

"Yup, I have a bag, if you don't mind."

"Of course." I slipped through the bushes just as Granddad was about to bring me the bag.

"Either you are in a rush, or I am getting slower in my old age."

"I am in a bit of a rush. I have this nagging feeling that I need to get to the dump quickly."

"Okay, well, here you go."

"Thanks." I threw the bag into my trunk then headed over to the dump.

As I pulled in, I saw Steve's truck parked over to the side. He was sorting his recyclables. I paid my bag fee, smiled, and waved at the attendant then drove through. No time to talk today as I needed to get over to Steve. Luckily, there was a spot next to his truck, so I quickly pulled in.

"Hello, stranger," I said in a friendly tone.

Steve popped his head up and glanced at me with a startled look. He obviously hadn't seen me at first. "Oh, hey, Evie."

"Hi, long time no see. How have you been?" When he had lifted his head, I could tell that he wasn't doing well. His disheveled clothes and the dark circles under his eyes told me everything.

He averted my gaze. "Um ... A lot has been going on. I've been trying to stay busy."

"Is there anything that I can help you with?"

"No, no. I'm good."

We worked in silence for a few minutes.

"Okay. Hey, I left you a voicemail. I was wondering if you received it."

"Yeah, sorry. Like I said, there has been a lot going on."

"I completely understand. Well, I don't want to trouble you. There is no need to get back to me. Take care." When I turned to walk away, I could tell he wanted to say something more, but he just lowered his head.

I got back in my car and slowly drove out of the dump, looking in my rearview mirror. Steve just kept his head down.

How am I going to run this program without him?

I took the scenic route home, driving by the beach and around the cliffs, trying to figure it all out. *Maybe Principal Patrick knows someone*, I thought.

Then I heard, *"Turn off your head and turn on your heart."*

"Huh?"

"Declare it, and it will be so."

"What? Declare what?"

"Declare what you want, and it will be."

Not understanding what was being asked of me, I parked at the cliffs and called my spiritual guru, Colbie, back in Denver. We hadn't connected since I had returned, so I owed her a call.

"Evie, hey, it's been a while."

"I know. I have been wanting to call you to catch up, but life happened."

"It always does."

"Do you have a few minutes?"

"Sure. So, what has been going on?"

"Things have been crazy since I last saw you in Denver."

"How so?"

"Well, first off, Hendrix proposed!"

"*What*? That is amazing news. Congratulations."

"Thank you."

"So, when is the wedding?"

"We haven't gotten that far yet. He has Aja, and I have Granddad. Neither can move right now, so we still have a good deal of logistics to work out."

"And I can tell there is something else. What is it?"

"Well, as I mentioned to you before, I don't know how we can make this work. Hendrix believes we can. I am still having a hard time seeing it."

"*Seeing it*? That may be the issue. Can you feel it in your heart that you and Hendrix will be together?"

"Yes, I can, but I don't know how we will get there." Just at that moment, a strong smell of cigarette smoke filled my nose. I looked around to see if there was someone else around, but then I realized it was my reminder.

"That is not for you to figure out. If you declare it, then it will be."

"What did you say?"

"If you declare it, it will be."

"Amazing. That is another reason I called. I was just told to do that with another issue, but I don't really know what it means."

"When you declare something, you know it will be, and you will do whatever it takes to make it so."

"How do I do that? Do I say it to him or—"

"No, you just need to say it to yourself. But you have to mean it and commit to doing whatever it takes to make it so. Do you remember when you laid me off from my job so many moons ago and I said *thank you*?"

"Yes, I thought that was the weirdest response I had ever heard."

"I knew Spirit was giving me the push that I needed to take a leap. I had dabbled in energy work and coaching, but I only did it for fun and to help friends. Deep down, I wanted to do this type of work full-time. Declaring that I could do this work and support my family was my commitment to myself, and I knew Spirit would guide me the entire way."

I let her words sink in. "Colbie, you are so good. No wonder you are killing it with your business. You just seem to know what I need and how to make me understand."

She laughed. "Don't think I do this all by myself. I have help."

"I hear you, and thank you. So, how are your two young men doing? Still weeds?"

"I swear, every morning, they look like they have grown. It's a good thing business is going well, because they are eating me out of house and home."

I laughed. "Well, I hope you all can visit this summer. My granddad would love to take them fishing."

"Oh, Evie, that would be wonderful. We will make it happen. I have just declared it."

It was so good to talk to Colbie. She was my spiritual rock, always knowing what I needed and delivering it in the most perfect way.

Driving back home, as I was coming down my road, I saw a truck parked in the driveway. As I got closer, I realized it was Steve.

I parked then walked over and looked through the truck window. He was just sitting there, staring off into the distance.

"Do you want to come in?" I asked. "I can make some coffee."

"Sure, thanks," he said gruffly.

I headed inside and, after a few moments, I heard Steve come up the stairs.

"Come on in."

He gave me a slight smile as he came in then took a seat at the kitchen table, keeping his head low. "Sorry for being short with you at the dump. I wasn't expecting to see you there."

"No worries. I know we have spoken little since I returned from Colorado."

"Yeah, about that." He glanced at me. "I just needed some time to lick my wounds." Shifting in the chair, he said, "I don't know why I thought a woman like you wouldn't be with someone."

Luckily, I was over at the stove, pouring the coffee, and not sitting in front of him. I didn't know what to say, so I said nothing.

I handed Steve a cup and slid the sugar and creamer over to him. He noticed my ring.

"Beautiful ring. He has great taste."

"Th-Thank you," I stammered.

We sat in silence for a few minutes, drinking our coffee. With each sip, I could see Steve slowly relax. However, his tension returned when he noticed me looking at him.

"So, you mentioned something about a program that you and Bill Frank were working on?"

"Yes, when I was teaching at the high school, I met a young man who really benefited from my painting program. It helped him process his emotions. He lost his mom and moved to the island to live with his grandparents."

"Huh. Did you tell him you went through the same thing?"

"Yes, that is how I thought of the program. Just like how painting has, and continues, to help me process my emotions, it helped him open up to his grandparents and process his grief. He confided in me that his mother had come to him in a dream, which freed him from the guilt that he had been carrying. Both Mr. Frank and I thought that, if we gave this opportunity to more kids, they would learn better ways to manage their emotions."

"Hey, out of curiosity, why do you call Bill Mr. Frank?"

I chuckled. "That is how I have always known him. I met him as a teenager, new to the island and high school. He was my teacher, and I never transitioned to calling him by his first name. Actually, I never knew his first name until you mentioned it."

"Well, I know you helped me process my emotions with your something-something painting technique, so I am sure you will do wonders with those kids."

"Thank you, but Mr. Frank—I mean, Bill—was going to be my partner in this program. I would teach painting, and he would be the counselor. Since he is no longer with us, I know he would want *you* to be a part of this program. Your name was the one and only name that came to me when I meditated on this."

"Whoa, whoa, Evie. I am no counselor. I am barely managing myself."

"That is exactly why you would be perfect. You can speak firsthand to these kids; let them learn from your life lessons. You can show them how painting from your heart or the something-something technique allows you to process and not run away from your emotions." I could see the doubt in Steve's eyes. "Steve, I was probably as unsure as you are now when you suggested last year that I teach the painting class at the high school. You saw something in me that I did not see. I took the leap and discovered that I could teach kids, and I actually enjoyed it."

"Bill told me you were amazing. The kids really gravitated to you."

I blushed. "Well, just like you saw something in me, I see something really special in you. You make everyone around you feel comfortable, and you are not afraid to share your feelings. Your life experiences can help others. You just have to believe you can do it."

Steve's eyes were heavy, but I could tell he was considering it.

"Please promise me that you will really think about this before you give me your answer. I need to get back to the principal in about a week or so to let her know if the program will be moving forward."

"Will the program continue if I don't do it?"

I shrugged. "Maybe."

"What do you mean, *maybe*?"

"Actually, it will. I just declared it. My hope is you will want to join me, but if you decide against it, I understand. The principal and I will work to find someone to fill that role."

Steve sat back in the chair and looked at me. He wasn't really looking at me. It felt more like he was looking through me, like he had gone somewhere else.

"All right," he eventually sighed out. "Give me a day, and I will get back to you."

"Thank you. I really appreciate you giving this some serious thought."

With that, Steve said his goodbyes and walked out.

CHAPTER 5 — WHAT FRIENDS DO

The photo shoot was scheduled, and I received the interview questions. I was surprised by how personal some of the questions were. Tatum would definitely need to help me answer some of them, but not particularly those questions.

Standing in front of my closet, I didn't know what I should wear for the photo shoot. Should I be moody, flowy, businesslike, pensive, or casual? Before I had left Denver, I had cut my closet down by three quarters, so the selection was limited. I decided on casual, so jeans and a simple V-neck patterned top would do the trick. Now, what would I do with my hair? It hadn't been cut in forever, so my bangs were grown out, and it was longer than I had ever worn it. Since we were shooting in a studio, I didn't have to worry about the weather jacking it up. I would just flat iron and hope for the best.

Last thing to focus on was makeup. Rummaging through my makeup bag, I checked the expiration dates on the bottles. Only a few months past the date, so I should be good … I hoped. Now, the next issue: did I remember how to put it on?

To ensure that I would be ready, I did a dry run with the outfit, hair, and makeup. I sent Hendrix a few selfies, and he was quick to respond with a heart-eyed emoji. Guessed he approved.

One last look in the mirror, and I was ready to wash my face and change my clothes. A knock on the door delayed my transition back.

"Evie, it's Steve. You home?"

"Yes, come on in. I'll be right out."

Coming out of my bedroom, I saw Steve looking at me from the front room.

"Wow!" His stare made me blush. "You look great."

"Uh … Thank you. I was doing a dry run for my photo shoot tomorrow."

"Photo shoot?"

"Yup, I needed a professional headshot for an interview that I am doing."

"Oh, really? Who's doing the shoot?"

"Judy B. Photography."

"Yeah, she's good. You know I could have done that for you. I took my cousin Beth's headshot."

I acted like I didn't know. "Really? Well, you have helped me more than enough times. I wouldn't have wanted to bother you."

Steve gave me a funny look then said, "That's what friends do, right? Help each other out."

Immediately, I felt like a jerk. I didn't even try to remove my foot from my mouth. All I said was, "Yes, that's what friends do."

"Well, I just came over to tell you that I will be your partner in the Something-Something Painting Program."

"You will?" I clapped my hands like a child who had just received some candy. "That is wonderful. Thank you."

Steve couldn't help but smile at my excitement.

"I will give the principal a call tomorrow to tell her the news, and I will email you the program overview. Thank you, Steve. This means so much to me, and I am sure that Mr. Frank—I mean, Bill—is smiling right now."

"He is the one who guided me to say yes."

"Wonderful."

***

Surprisingly, the photo shoot went well. Judy made me feel comfortable, and she caught my natural smile. Now that that was done, I needed to work on the interview questions.

I texted Tatum.

Headshot done. Can we chat? I need to work on the interview questions.

Most of the questions were pretty run of the mill—*when did you start painting? who was your biggest influence? what is your style?*—but the question about the commission piece made me somewhat uneasy. I could understand the desire to want to know about the inspiration for the piece, but I didn't want to share my family's dirty laundry. I hoped Tatum could help me with that.

I sat at the kitchen table, typing the answers to the easy interview questions, but I was still stuck on the inspiration question for the commission piece. How did you sum up a lifetime of emotional issues into a few sentences without throwing your family under the bus?

I closed my eyes and gently placed my fingers on the keyboard. One deep breath grounded me, and then I waited until something came to me.

> *Painting is an emotional experience for me. Generally, it allows me to relive the emotion that I felt when I first experienced the inspiration. Other times, painting serves as my therapy. It allows me to release the emotions that are no longer serving me. It gives me a judgment-free space to just let it all go.*
>
> *The inspiration for this piece was just that—my therapy. I was finally letting go of emotions that I had allowed to eat at me for far too long. Once those emotions were released, I could move forward and understand the reasons behind why I had those emotions to begin with.*

It sounded pretty good.

I completed the rest of the questions then sent my answers off the Tatum. Soon thereafter, she responded.

> *Sorry I wasn't able to call. Been in meetings all day. Reviewed your answers and love them, particularly the inspiration question. You are getting good at this stuff. I am sure they will like your answers, but they will still want the opportunity to chat just in case they need some clarification. I will send video call information as soon as I confirm with them.*

She closed out her text with a thumbs-up emoji.

***

I had been so focused on the Bali tourism interview that I hadn't given the Something-Something Painting Program much thought. It thrilled the high school principal, Susan Patrick, to know that the program would be moving forward. We would start the last quarter of the school year as a test run then evaluate over the summer to see what, if any, changes should be made or if the program would continue. That gave me a little less than a month to pull this together with Steve and submit the overview to the counselors. We hadn't spoken since he had agreed to work with me, so I sent him a text to schedule a meeting.

Steve, are you available this week to plan for the Something-Something Program? Was thinking dinner with Granddad when you have time. Let me know.

Tomorrow night works. Seven o'clock?

Perfect.

Meeting set, now I needed to develop a program overview for the counselors. Back again at my computer.

Funny how, only a few years ago, all I had done was write on my computer. Eight hours straight, I would sit in front of a screen. Now I had to dust off my laptop before I used it.

An enormous smile crossed my face. *Ha, how my life has changed for the better.*

Again, I closed my eyes and placed my fingers on the keyboard, waiting for words to come to me.

The Something-Something Painting Program was developed to support youth in the processing and management of their emotions. Teenagers are up against many factors that can impact their emotional wellbeing. Social, family, financial, physical, and emotional issues, if not managed, can turn into a perfect storm, affecting a young person's confidence and mental state, which can unfortunately lead to bad life choices.

The late Mr. Bill Frank and I have experience in poor decision-making that has impacted our lives. Prior to his death, Bill worked hard, through counseling, to manage his emotions, to accept his mistakes, and worked with others to do the same. In my own process, painting has allowed me to release old beliefs, work through my emotions, and accept myself as who I am but knowing I can create the life I desire. He and I wanted to let young people know that, with guidance, they can change the course of their lives and deal with their emotions now rather than have them impact how they live their lives in the future.

The program has two components: 1) painting, and 2) counseling. Teachers and administrators may recommend that a student attend this program or students can opt in themselves. Two days a week, after school, painting and counseling will be available.

The purpose is not to develop accomplished painters out of the students, but to allow them to use painting as a release from their pent-up emotions. For some, that may be enough, but for others, group or individual counseling may be incorporated.

> *I will teach painting, and the counseling program will be led by Steve Rice. The program will be offered the last quarter of this school year as a test run with evaluation throughout the summer to determine if the program will continue the following school year.*

With my hand on my heart center, I gave appreciation for the guidance. *Well, thank you for that.* The program sounded fantastic, but just to be sure, I sent the draft to Josh, my former painting class student who served as the impetus for the program, to see if he approved.

Shoot, it was almost five o'clock and I hadn't started dinner. Tonight was movie night with Granddad, and he liked to eat early.

I rummaged through the refrigerator to find the chicken thighs that I had marinated in adobe sauce. Spicy. I made some rice, heated a can of black beans, and warmed the tortillas on the stove. By the time Granddad walked in, the house smelled delicious.

"So, what movie are we watching tonight?" I asked.

"Something special."

"I'm intrigued."

"What smells so good?"

"Hope you are up for spicy."

"Always good to add a little spice. Cleans the pipes and keeps the ole ticker ticking."

"Wow, TMI, but I am happy that you are game."

Granddad set the table, and I served dinner.

"I always love when you make new dishes. I'm an old fisherman who could eat chowder every night. You are opening my taste buds."

"It's nice to cook for someone else, and I am glad you enjoy it. Can we do this again tomorrow night? I have invited Steve over to discuss the Something-Something Painting Program, and I would love for you to help in the planning."

"Well, I guess he wasn't too hurt that you are marrying another man."

"Granddad!"

He laughed. "I'm glad you guys sorted everything out and he is working with you on this. What time?"

"Seven o'clock. Is that too late for you to eat?"

"If you are going to make something this good again, I can wait."

Granddad cleaned his plate so well that it didn't even look like he had used it.

"Phew, that was delicious. I will feel this later, but it was worth it."

We cleared the dishes, and I put the kettle on to make us some tea while we watched the movie.

"So, what's the name of the movie?"

"Can't tell."

"Why?"

"Because it doesn't have one. Just sit down and enjoy."

Granddad put the disc in the DVD player, and then an image slowly appeared. It was a still photo of Granddad when he was much younger, dressed in full Native American regalia. As the pictures continued to appear, I witnessed Granddad and tribal members at the local powwow, fishing, quahogging, and participating in Cranberry Day celebrations. Then there were pictures of some men making a structure.

"What are they building?" I asked.

"It's a wetu, or house. This is traditionally what we lived in. It's made out of saplings and tree bark."

The final images were tribal members burning out a log. "Why are they burning that log?"

"It's in preparation for carving it into a canoe."

"Granddad, who made this?"

"I did."

"Really? When did you do this?"

"It was just finished. I worked with our cultural center to put it together. They had a bunch of old pictures that I wanted you to see. They were kind enough to load them onto this DVD. My hope is that it would be a good way for you to learn more about our ways."

"This is absolutely wonderful."

For the rest of the evening, Granddad told me stories that were so vivid that it was like I was transported back in time and was witnessing everything firsthand.

"Hey, have you received anything from the tribe yet?" he suddenly asked.

"Funny you should ask. I just got something yesterday. It's still in my pile of mail."

"Well, open it up."

I walked over to the table and rifled through the mail.

"Gee, haven't opened your mail in a while, huh?"

"I always seem to get sidetracked. Oh, here it is." I opened the envelope and unfolded the letter, reading the contents to myself. Then I looked at Granddad with a smile on my face. "I am officially enrolled in the tribe."

Granddad gave me a huge hug. "Your father and I have wanted to do this for you for a very long time. I am sorry it took so long."

"Please, Granddad, don't be sorry. I wasn't ready before, but I am now. What is this? My enrollment number is 1522? What does that mean?"

"It represents that you are the one thousand five hundred and twenty-second person to be enrolled in the tribe. You need that number for tribal voting and other things. Don't worry about that now. I'm just happy that you are finally enrolled."

After Granddad left, I washed the dishes and thought about the evening. Such a fascinating experience. It was like all the pieces were coming together. The energy within me was flowing, and I needed to paint what I was feeling.

It was late, and the studio was cold, so I made a fresh cup of tea to warm myself.

As I stared at the canvas, a flood of emotions filled me. So much history and culture. Times were hard, but tribal members stayed together, helping each other out.

The pallet was black, white, and grey with pops of red to represent the cranberries. Images of days gone by. Faces of old and young. Normally, I painted in abstract, but Granddad's stories were so vivid that I needed to paint in detail to create the same realism that I had felt when hearing his stories.

When I stopped, several hours had passed. It was early morning now, and I needed to get some rest. The painting wasn't complete, but I had been able to capture most of the emotions that I had felt from the evening.

***

When I opened my eyes, the sun was streaming into my bedroom. What time was it? I grabbed my phone and realized it was almost eleven-thirty. I had a voicemail, texts, and emails. Wow, busy morning. First things first, I called Hendrix.

"Hey, I have been worried about you. Didn't hear from you last night or this morning. Everything okay?"

"Yes, sorry. Granddad and I had dinner last night, and he surprised me with a DVD collage of old photos. The energy that I received from the pictures and his stories inspired me to paint, so I painted until the wee hours of the morning. Sorry to have worried you."

"All I ask is that you text, then I will know not to bother you."

"*Bother me*? I love hearing from you."

"Even when you're painting?"

"Well ... all right, I promise I will text next time. How is Aja doing?"

"She is fantastic, as usual. Healthy and happy, just like a little girl should be."

"And her mom?"

"No change there."

"Oh. Well, I have some good news to share."

"Really?"

"Yes, I am now a member of the tribe. Received my letter the other day. My tribal enrollment number is 1522."

"Enrollment number?"

"Yeah, I know. I had to ask Granddad about that, as well."

"Well, congratulations."

"Also, we are moving forward with the Something-Something Painting Program. Steve and Granddad are coming over for dinner tonight to help plan."

"Nice. Things are really moving in the right direction. I am so proud of you. Your painting technique and guidance will help a lot of young people."

"Thank you."

"Okay, beautiful, I have to run. Talk to you tonight. Love you."

"Love you, too!"

I rolled out of bed and headed into the bathroom. When I looked in the mirror, I screamed. There was a big red splotch on my face. *Did something bite me?* I reached up to touch the area and realized it was paint from last night. Wow, was I out of it.

I washed my face then headed to the kitchen to make coffee. While it brewed, I had the breakfast of champions—a big bowl of cereal—and sat at the table while reading my emails. Great, Josh liked the write-up and would vouch for the program if any of the counselors asked him. He was so sweet. Tatum had also emailed the video call information. Two-thirty in the morning. *Ugh.* I purposely stayed away from reading the news and ate the rest of my breakfast, or brunch, in silence.

The day flew by, but I guessed that happened when you didn't wake up until after eleven o'clock. To prepare for tonight's dinner and meeting, I made a pan full of meatballs and let them simmer in a simple tomato sauce. I didn't want to make anything crazy, so spaghetti and meatballs would do the trick. Then I set the table before jumping in the shower.

Granddad was the first to arrive.

"Mmm ... Smells good in here. Last night, Mexican, and tonight, Italian?"

"I like to shake things up."

"Come on in," Granddad unexpectedly announced, making me jump.

Steve opened the door, shaking his head. "How do you do that?"

Granddad simply laughed.

"Wow, it smells great in here. I brought dessert—brownies."

"Oh, my favorite!" I proclaimed. "All good thinking food. Grab what you want to drink from the fridge."

Steve and Granddad took their seats, and I served. We all jumped right in and ate in silence for about five minutes before I asked if everything was okay. Granddad gave me thumbs-up, and Steve nodded.

After the feeding frenzy had subsided, I offered seconds. Both eagerly accepted.

"Thanks for joining me tonight. Steve, the principal was so pleased to hear that we were moving forward with the program. We agreed we would do a test run the last semester of the year, and then evaluate over the summer, which means we have about a month before the program is live. Granddad, since you have been sponsoring and helping people your whole life, I wanted your input on the program, as well."

He nodded. "Always happy to help."

"I took the liberty of drafting an overview of the program for the counselors so they will know what to expect."

After reading the overview, both agreed it sounded good.

"You obviously have the painting portion down, but how should we run the counseling?" Steve asked.

"At first, I don't think we will have a lot of kids in the program, so we can take our time and feel it out."

"I would suggest that you ask the referring counselor to complete an intake form so that you both know what you are working with. In my experience, young people are not that forthcoming, so you may have to pry it out of them."

"Good idea, Attaquin," Steve replied. "I was also thinking that it would be the young person's choice if they wanted to start with painting or with counseling."

"Yes, they will want to feel in control of the situation. No one likes having things forced on them, particularly when it is so personal," Granddad added.

The rest of the evening, we ate brownies—the entire pan, to be exact—and brainstormed the program. The energy amongst us was amazing. It thrilled us to know we were creating something that could really help kids.

At the end of the night, Granddad and I walked Steve out to his truck. Before he drove away, he rolled down his window. "Evie, thank you for bullying me—oh, I mean, *asking* me—to be a part of this program. It makes me feel fantastic that I can help a young person avoid some of the mistakes I made."

"Sometimes, it takes strong persuasion for us to see what is so apparent to others," I replied.

"Oh, and Attaquin, I am sure we have room for another counselor if you would consider joining the team."

"That's a great idea. Granddad, would you help us?"

"Let me think about it. The young ones don't always want to hear from us old folks."

"But remember, Granddad, you are not old, just wise."
"Steve, be careful with this one. She is good."
"I know. Believe me, I know."

CHAPTER 6 — BIG GIRL PANTS

At two fifteen in the morning, I was dressed, hair done, and makeup on. With a hot cup of coffee, I reviewed the answers that I had submitted to the *Best Bali* tourism magazine one more time. Then, to make sure that I was on time, I joined the video call early. Another participant had joined, so it must have been Tatum. She got it easy. It was only twelve thirty at night for her.

I texted her, *Good morning.*

You ready? she asked.

As ready as I will ever be.

Great. Please remember to have fun and smile.

Just as I was about to respond, the video call was opened. A tall, slender man and a small woman who had the most radiant complexion appeared on the screen. Both had welcoming smiles. I could also see Tatum in a smaller screen off to the side.

"Good afternoon, Ms. Prince. My name is Nyoman, and, I along with my coworker, Ni Kadek, are the writers of the *Best Bali* magazine."

Ni Kadek nudged Nyoman.

"Excuse me, I guess I should say *good morning*."

"Good morning, and please, call me Evie. Thank you both for this opportunity. I am sure you remember Tatum Brown, my agent."

"Of course. Hello, Tatum," Ni Kadek greeted.

"It is so nice to put a face to a name. I would like to reiterate Evie's sentiment. We really appreciate this opportunity."

"It is our honor. There has been a lot of excitement around the grand opening of our newest hotel on Bali, and the piece you painted, Evie, was the crowning jewel of an amazing hotel."

"Thank you. I really appreciate the compliment and look forward to the day when I can visit the hotel to see it myself."

"Well, when you come to visit, please make sure that you call us. Nyoman and I would love to show you around."

"Yes, we would," Nyoman replied. "And thank you. We received your responses to our questions. We just have a few follow-up questions that we would like to ask you."

Immediately, panic filled me.

"Evie, is everything okay?" Nyoman asked. He must have seen the fear on my face.

"Yes." I quickly pulled myself together and put a smile back on my face. "What can I clarify for you?"

"Your website bio mentions that you tried painting when you were younger, but you could not make a living at it. Was there something that made this time different?"

Wow, did not see that one coming.

There was a momentary pause as I closed my eyes and took a deep breath. Then a smile unconsciously crossed my face. "I would like to say that the pandemic changed my life. It forced me to take the time to listen to myself. I was living my life to please everyone but me. When I realized that, it also became clear what made me happy. Painting has always been my passion, and once I started using the something-something technique, my paintings connected with more people."

I could see a bit of confusion on both of their faces. Then Ni Kadek responded with, "The something-something technique? Can you please explain more?"

I laughed, realizing that the not-so-technical name for my process would soon be made public to the people of Bali and Indonesia. "The something-something technique is when I paint through my heart versus my eyes. When I was younger, I painted what I saw in front of me. Now, I paint how I feel. If someone were to look at my paintings, then look at the object that I was painting, they would not be the same thing. The emotion I feel is what I paint." Out of the corner of my eye, I saw a clapping emoji come across my phone screen. I guessed Tatum liked that answer.

"Oh, I understand. Well, the emotion that you put into your painting definitely leapt off the canvas. One more question," Ni Kadek stated. "Will you be doing additional paintings for the hotel?"

"At this moment, no. But I would love to have the opportunity to work with Mr. Pratama again."

"Well, thank you, Evie, for your time. We really appreciate speaking with you."

"We will send Tatum copies of the magazine when the article prints," Nyoman added.

After we said our goodbyes, Tatum called me.

"Well done. And you said that you didn't enjoy talking about yourself."

"Like I said, I had to put on my big girl pants."

"It went great. I hope you are pleased."

"Actually, I am."

"Remember, every time, it will get easier and easier."

"*Every time?*" There was going to be more?

Back when I had been in corporate America, I could talk about any project, product, or company ad nauseum, but now, having to talk about myself just sent me into a tailspin.

"Oh, you think this is your one and only magazine interview? Trust me; there will be more."

The thought of more interviews scared the crap out of me, but there was also a small part of me that looked forward to the next one.

I waited until the morning to let Hendrix know how the interview went.

"Good morning, beautiful."

"Good morning. Great news. The interview was a success."

"Wonderful. Did you smile?"

"Gee, do you and Tatum think that I always have a sour puss face?"

"No, but when you get anxious, your smile goes away. It's noticeable."

"Huh, good to know. And yes, I did smile. So, what is on your agenda today?"

"Remember when we first met and I was contemplating stepping away from corporate headhunting and going out on my own?"

"Yes."

"Do you also remember that you suggested I should be a passion hunter versus a headhunter?"

"I do."

"Well, I have been thinking a lot more about it. I still enjoy the work, but—"

"How exciting!" I shrieked.

"What?" Hendrix laughed. "I haven't even told you everything yet."

"I don't care what you are going to tell me. I am just happy that you are taking another leap toward your happiness. So, tell me, what are you going to do?" I asked excitedly.

"Well, I need more flexibility for Aja, and hitting my numbers every month wears on me." He paused and laughed again. "Right there just proves why I love you so much—unconditional love and support. Honestly, I was a little nervous about telling you that I'm starting the process of creating my own company."

"Why would you be nervous? I turned down my dream job that you found for me, sold my house, and moved to another state within a six-month period. I understand the need for change."

"Yes, but we were not engaged. We were just friends with the hope—at least for me—for more. What I do now impacts you and vice versa."

"Hendrix, I would never dream of standing in your way of happiness. And Aja needs you."

"Thank you. Oh, and my official title is Passion Hunter. Still need to think of a name for the business, but I will be helping people find their passion, and then their perfect job that fulfills their passion."

"That sounds amazing, and I know you will have people from everywhere wanting to work with you. Congratulations. Is there anything that I can do to help?"

"Just keep on being you. Your support gives me the strength to keep moving forward."

***

Thinking about marrying Hendrix frightened and excited me at the same time. My maternal grandfather had spent his whole life trying to keep me safe, fearful that I would follow in his and my mother's footsteps, and concerned that my free spirit would put me in harm's way.

Humanitarian work overseas, like my mother and grandfather had done, did not interest me, but I did have the urge to wander. I wanted to see the sights and hear the sounds of the world. Would marrying Hendrix keep me from that, or would he encourage it?

When Granddad entered the studio, he cleared his throat to announce his arrival. He could probably tell that I was in deep thought.

"Oh, Granddad, I didn't hear you come in."

"Sorry, kid, I knocked."

"Yeah, I was a little preoccupied."

"Anything I can help you with?"

"Remember how you told me that my free spirit frightened my grandfather because he thought I would put myself in danger like my mother?"

"Yes ... Where is this going?" he asked cautiously.

"Don't worry; I'm not going to follow in their footsteps, but I do feel the need to wander."

"What is wrong with that? To see the world and how other people live is an amazing experience that everyone should have. If more did, there may be more love in this world."

"I am just concerned that, when Hendrix and I marry, we cannot do that, since Aja is so young."

"Have you spoken to him about this, or are you letting your mind run wild, worrying about things that aren't even real yet?"

I lowered my head, knowing that Granddad was right. Then the slight scent of cigarette smoke filled my nose. My head and ego had taken control, and I was worrying about something that I had no business worrying about.

Sheepishly, I replied, "No, not yet."

"Well, these are important topics that you need to discuss with Hendrix. Try not to limit yourself and think that there is only this *or* that. It can be this *and* that, if you make it so."

I got up from my stool to give Granddad a hug.

"Whoa. What is this for?"

"Thank you for being you. I know you all sacrificed a lot for me. I am just so happy to have you with me on this journey."

"Evie, we did not sacrifice. Your maternal grandparents, your mother, father, and I made choices, choices that we thought were in your best interest. If we were given a do-over, we would choose you and your safety again."

***

That evening, before bed, I sat out on the deck and looked at the lighthouse. Red, red, white. Her soothing light lulled me, as if she were rocking me to sleep, like how my mother used to when I was a small child.

My mother and I had had a complicated relationship, but I always knew that she had loved me. My best memories were of when I was young, before she would leave and I was sent to stay with my grandparents. She would shower me with love. We would cuddle on the couch and just *be* for hours together. Those memories gave me a warm sensation throughout my body and a sense of peace.

I closed my eyes, appreciating the stillness. Then, in the back of my head, I felt a familiar presence.

"*I am so proud of you, Evie.*"

"Mom? Is that you?"

"*Yes, sweetheart. It's me.*"

At that moment, it was like a dam broke. Tears streamed from my eyes, and I was inundated with emotion. The last time I had spoken with my mother had been two weeks before she had died. It had been twenty-five years since I had heard her voice.

"Mom, I miss you."

"*I know, and I am sorry. Please know I am always with you.*"

"I know, but it still hurts."

"*The pain that you feel when you miss a loved one provides you with the understanding to appreciate the people you love in your life. Without sadness, you cannot know happiness.*"

"Mom, I have done a lot of work to understand the choices that you all made regarding me, but one thing I still don't understand is how you could leave me to help other children around the world. Didn't you love me?"

"*Evie, it was hard to leave you, but I knew you would be well taken care of. The desire in my heart to help those in need was too great to ignore. The more I pushed that desire aside, the unhappier I became. I was a better person to you, and everyone else, when I could be me and do the things that brought me joy.*

"*And, of course I loved you. More than you can imagine. The months that I would be away from you to help others were difficult, but the work gave me immense joy. I brought that joy home to you. If I was not allowed to do my humanitarian work, I feared I would grow to resent you. With the help of your grandparents, I could do what I loved and still be with the one person who I loved more than myself."*

"Mom, I love Hendrix, and I want to be with him, but I also have an unrelenting desire to see the world."

"Evie, you need to be you and do what makes you happy. If you want to be with Hendrix, you will. The timing may just differ from what you think. In the end, you will be a better person to him, and yourself, because you are being your true self."

"I wonder if Hendrix can't wait. I wonder if I'll lose him."

"Be strong in your decisions. Maybe he does not want to wait, but wouldn't it be better to live your authentic life than to live a lie and be unhappy?"

"Yes, I understand. Thank you, Mom. I love you."

"I love you, too, sweetheart. Remember, I am always with you."

Feeling her presence was so loving that I didn't want it to end.

When I opened my eyes, I saw the red, red, white beams of light and realized that the lighthouse represented my mother—strong, distant, loving, and always there to guide me.

CHAPTER 7 — MAGIC IN A CUP

In a few days, Hendrix and I would finally be together again. Thinking about him sent shivers throughout my body. There was so much that I wanted to show and share with him.

I cleaned the house and studio, went food shopping, and got my supply of movies from the library. Not like we wouldn't be doing other things at night, but I wanted to make sure that everything was perfect.

Prior to picking him up, I checked myself and my outfit for what seemed like the millionth time before I jumped into the car. It was still early in the season, so traffic was not bad. I found a great parking spot and waited in my car until the boat docked. One more check in the rearview mirror and I was ready to greet my fiancé.

Waiting for the passengers to unload, I could feel my heart beating out of my chest. Nervousness and excitement were coursing through my veins. Finally, I saw him. There weren't many people waiting, so I knew he saw me immediately. His smile was like a beam of light aimed right at me. I tried to stay put, but I couldn't. Just as he stepped off the platform, I launched myself at him, barely giving him time to drop his bag. We didn't even notice if anyone was around or if we were in the way. Everything seemed like it was in slow motion, which made our embrace and kiss even more exhilarating. Slowly, Hendrix then placed me on the ground.

"Hello, beautiful."

I blushed. "It feels so good to finally have you here with me."

"It feels so good to finally be here."

"Are you tired? I thought we could do a little sightseeing?"

"Being with you, I have all the energy in the world."

We put his bag in the car, and then we walked around town, hand in hand, window shopping and sightseeing. It was like something magnetically attached us to each other. I had always negatively judged couples who walked around completely intertwined, arms around waists or in back pockets, thinking how uncomfortable and impractical that was, but now I was doing it and fully enjoying it. At times, it was a little awkward, but I just couldn't keep my hands off of him.

After about an hour, I could tell Hendrix's travel was catching up to him, so we grabbed a cup of coffee from my favorite bakery for the drive back up island. We would do more sightseeing another day. All I wanted to do was be with Hendrix.

As we drove up the road to the house, I saw Granddad coming out. Knowing we caught him red-handed, he waited until we parked.

"I was trying to surprise you, but you got home sooner than I thought."

"Granddad, you remember Hendrix."

"Of course, my soon-to-be grandson-in-law."

Hendrix walked over to Granddad to shake his hand, but Granddad pulled him in for a hug, to both our surprises.

"Nice to see you again, Hendrix. Thank you for making my granddaughter so happy."

"Sir, it is my pleasure. She is an amazing woman, and her love has given me the strength to do things I didn't know I could."

"Yeah, she is that good," Granddad said with a smile. "So, I was trying to be sneaky and drop off some lobsters. They are in your chiller."

"Thank you, Granddad."

"Okay. I will leave you two. Hendrix, have a wonderful visit."

"Thank you, sir."

"Please, call me Attaquin."

We brought Hendrix's bag and a few items we got at the store into the house. Once we put everything away, I looked at Hendrix. "Are you hungry?"

"No, but I would love to take a shower."

"Of course. Towels and everything are in the bathroom."

I thought about cooking the lobsters so they would be ready when he came out of the shower, but then I had a better idea.

I knocked lightly on the bathroom door.

"Yes?"

"Would you like company?"

"I thought you'd never ask."

***

Lying next to Hendrix put me in a peaceful place. To hear him breathe and to feel his chest rise and fall must have been how a baby felt in the womb when they could hear their mother's heartbeat—safe and comfortable.

I awoke to the smell of coffee and bacon. Smiling, I gave appreciation for my wonderful life.

"Good morning, beautiful. I made you some coffee."

"Is it the special coffee that you still haven't shown me how to make?"

"Of course."

I sat up in bed and gratefully accepted what I believed was magic in a cup. The smell was just different. I didn't know how he made it, but it was the best cup of coffee that I had ever drank. Still hot, I took small sips, each one warming my body.

"So, I have bacon and eggs ready when you are."

"Wow, the royal treatment." I shuffled out of the room with my coffee cup still in hand and settled in at the kitchen table.

Hendrix had a grace about him that you would not expect from such a big man, and he definitely knew his way around a kitchen. I quietly watched him work, admiring his every move. *How did I get so lucky?* I thought to myself.

Hendrix caught me watching him. "What?"

"I am just appreciating my soon-to-be husband."

As he placed my breakfast in front of me, he said, "Thank you for the appreciation, my soon-to-be wife."

Hearing him say that sent a surge of energy through me, making me shiver.

"Are you cold? Do you want a sweater?"

"Ha, no, I'm good. Hearing you say that gave me wonderful shivers. I know we can make this work."

"Yes, we can."

After breakfast, I gave Hendrix a tour of the Sunshine Studio and my latest paintings. Then I took him over to the tribal office. We enjoyed a day of touring around the island and ended the day bundled up on the beach, watching the sunset.

"Evie, I want to make sure that you're okay with me moving forward with my new company."

"I am crazy excited and proud of you. I support your decision one hundred percent. You need to do what is best for you and Aja."

"Don't you mean for us and Aja?"

I didn't respond.

"Evie, you all right?"

"Yes. Sorry, that was the first time I thought of us as a family. I mean … That didn't come out right." Nothing was coming out of my mouth right, so I just closed it and sat there quietly.

"Beautiful, I know what you mean. This is all new for me, as well." He gave me a huge hug, and then we headed home.

That night in bed, before falling asleep, the cigarette smoke returned. Thoughts were racing through my head. Everything we did moving forward, we did as a team. My decisions impacted Hendrix and his me.

"Hendrix, you awake?" I whispered.

"Now I am." He rolled over and spooned me. "What's up, beautiful?"

"Will you travel the world with me?"

"I would love to, but …"

"But, what?" I rolled over to see his face.

"Evie, is this something that you want to do soon? There's still is a lot that I am managing with Aja and her mother's health."

"I know. I'm sorry," I replied quietly.

"Evie, what? What is it?"

"I am feeling this urge to travel and see the world, and I would love to do it with you."

"And I would love to join you, but if you are looking to do it soon, I cannot guarantee that I can go with you. Is there something going on? Have you been offered something?"

"No and no. I was just thinking." Now the smell of smoke was full-on. It was like Hendrix took a long drag on a cigarette and had blown it directly into my face. I stroked his cheek. "Don't worry, Hendrix. It's nothing. Let's get some sleep." I kissed him gently. "I love you."

I closed my eyes, but I could feel him searching my face, trying to figure out what was going on.

"Okay, let's talk more tomorrow. I love you, too."

***

At breakfast, Hendrix could feel my agitation.

"Would you like to talk?" he asked.

"I have been smelling smoke again."

"Do you know why?"

"Yes, it's us."

"What do you mean, *it's us*?"

"I am worried about how we are going to make this work."

"Evie, I know we have things to figure out, but I don't want you to worry. When you say *make this work*, what exactly do you mean? Is there a particular timeline that we are working on?"

"No ... not really. But I always thought that, when you got engaged, you get married within a year ... ish. Plus, where are we going to live? Here, or Denver, or somewhere else? And what about Aja? She needs you, and I know you can't be without her."

"Whoa, whoa, whoa. Evie, slow down. No wonder you are smelling smoke. Your mind is going a million miles a minute. Take a breath and close your eyes." He waited until I was calmer. "Now, what does your heart say? How do you feel?"

"My heart says that I want to live my life with you. I want you, Aja, and I to be a family."

"And that feels good to you?"

"Yes, it does."

"Then it will be. We don't need to live by other's rules. We make our own. Please remember this is our life and no one else's."

As soon as Hendrix said those words, I remembered what I had told Reva when she had concerns about having a big wedding. *"Whose wedding is it? Do what is right for you and Brian."* It had been Brian's family's expectations to have a large wedding, not theirs, and in the end, they had happily eloped. I needed to practice what I preached.

The recognition that I was more concerned about what others thought than what was good for us smacked me upside the head. *Ego, you are at it again.* Slowly, the cigarette smell dissipated.

It was really weird how that smell would come and go. Sometimes, I didn't realize that it was gone until I smelled it again. Then I needed to focus on why it had returned. Admittedly, this was not an enjoyable process, but I could finally appreciate its purpose.

The rest of Hendrix's stay was smoke-free. We had a wonderful time just being with each other. Our bond continued to grow, and it felt so warm and comforting. It had become clear to me why Hendrix had been so focused on learning to love himself first before committing to me. He was so confident and secure in us. Now that I knew how to love me first, I could also be secure in my relationship with Hendrix.

CHAPTER 8 — SPECIAL FRIEND

Today was the big day. In my morning meditation, I gave my appreciation to Mr. Frank and asked that he guide Steve and me through today's session. Steve picked me up, and then we headed down to the high school. A brief meeting with the counselors and the principal prior to the session would give us a better understanding of the young people who would be in attendance. Principal Patrick opened the meeting.

"Evie and Steve, please let me thank you both again for your willingness and generosity to the young people of the island. This program is truly out of the box for us, but we believe it will have a great impact on the students."

"It is our pleasure," Steve responded. "I know firsthand how this helps, and thanks to Evie and her patience, she has helped me process and manage my emotions from my childhood trauma."

"Evie, Steve, my name is Ben, and I am the counselor for this year's freshman class. I asked a young lady by the name of JoAnn to see you today. Very unstable childhood, which resulted in her being removed from her family, she moved to the island late last year to be fostered by one of our island families. She is very smart and creative but has angry outbursts that are extremely volatile."

"Do you know if she has ever painted before?" I asked.

"Not that I am aware, but as I mentioned, she is very creative."

"Good afternoon. I'm Sharon, a counselor for the senior class. The student that I asked to attend your session is named David. For the past three years, David was an excellent student—attended his classes, got good grades—but this year, something happened. He skips school often, doesn't turn in his work, and as such will fail his classes. He used to talk about college, but now he has become distant."

"Thank you all for this information, and thank you for the trust you are putting in us to help your students. We will let you know how it goes," I replied.

As soon as we left the room, everything became extremely real. *I know this process can help people, but I hope we are not in over our heads.*

I looked at Steve as we walked down the hall in silence. His face showed the same seriousness. Luckily, we arrived in the art room before JoAnn and David.

After closing the door, I took a deep breath then turned to Steve. "Thank you again for being my partner in this."

"Of course. I have a funny feeling we will be helped just as much as they will."

The bell rang, and soon thereafter, JoAnn entered the room. She was a petite young woman with an attitude that screamed *don't mess with me.*

"You must be JoAnn. My name is Evie, and this is Steve."

JoAnn looked us both up and down. "Hey."

"Why don't you take a seat at that table while we wait for the other student?" I could see the concern on JoAnn's face when

I said another student was joining us. "Don't worry; we are going to have some fun."

A few moments later, David strolled in.

"Hi, David. My name is Evie, this is Steve, and that is JoAnn. Glad you could make it."

He gave no reply and just sat down.

I started the conversation by summarizing the program, how they were the first, and that we would learn together as we went along.

"Did either of you know Mr. Bill Frank?"

"Yeah, I did. He was a good guy. He listened," David said.

"Well, Mr. Frank used to be my teacher when I moved to the island to live with my grandparents after my mother's death. He was a good friend to me, and he and I created this program. Prior to his death, he mentored Steve, so we have both experienced the magic of Mr. Frank."

Steve gave an overview of his background.

"So, you're not a psychiatrist or trained counselor?" JoAnn asked.

"No, I am not, but I have made enough mistakes in my life to teach others how to not make the same ones. Plus, I am still making mistakes, but now I know when I am doing it and why. To me, I am making progress in the right direction."

His answer seemed to impress both the kids. We were off to a good start.

I looked at JoAnn and David. "So, why did you agree to come to this program?"

"I thought I had to," JoAnn replied.

"I promised my mom I would come," David answered.

"Have either of you painted before?"

Both shook their heads.

"No worries. The purpose of teaching you how to paint is not to become an artist; it is to help you free your emotions and put them in a place that is safe. There is no critiquing your work. I will show you techniques, and then ask that you be honest with yourself. I want you to paint your emotions—good, bad, or otherwise. Steve is here to help you think about the emotions that you put on the canvas and how you can manage those emotions. Moving forward, we are a big team. Everything in this room stays in this room. We are here to create a safe space for all of us to manage what we are going through."

Four easels were set in a circle so no one could see the other's work. I showed David and JoAnn a few paint mixing techniques and strokes then asked them to think about an experience that they had recently had.

"What I would like you to do is to paint what you felt from that experience. For example, if I were to think about what I had for dessert last night, the colors would be happy and fun because I had my favorite ice cream—strawberry. But I may also include a few big circles of round things to show that even though I loved ice cream, if I eat too much, I will get fat. Your painting does not need to make sense to anyone but you. Use this as a release."

For the next thirty minutes, the room was quiet. Steve got right to work, whereas JoAnn and David took longer. I spoke to each of them individually, assuring them that this was a safe place and that, when they released the emotion, they would feel lighter. Slowly, JoAnn started to paint. David was still hesitant, but he eventually put something on the canvas.

We had a few moments before the session ended, so I asked Steve if he would share his painting with us.

"Sure." He turned his easel around for all of us to see.

Looking at JoAnn and David, I asked, "What emotions do you feel from looking at Steve's painting?"

"To me, it feels like happiness, then sadness, then ... nothing," JoAnn answered.

"Wow, JoAnn, you are very perceptive," Steve complimented.

"David, do you feel anything from Steve's painting?" I asked.

"It's not nothingness. I feel resolution."

"Either you guys got into my head, or my artistic ability has improved," Steve commented.

"Great job. Please know, David and JoAnn, that we would not expect you to share your work unless you felt comfortable doing so," I explained.

JoAnn raised her hand.

"Please, JoAnn, no need to raise your hand."

"Oh, okay. Is it okay if we ask what experience Steve painted?"

We all looked at Steve.

"Sure," Steve answered. "This was an experience that I just went through. I met someone who is really special. I thought she could be someone I could spend my life with. Unfortunately, she had met someone before me. It crushed me, and I fell into a bit of a depression and seriously contemplated doing some harmful stuff to myself. But this person is so special that I realized I would rather have them in my life as a friend who makes me a better person than to be mad about something that wasn't meant to be."

As my face flushed, I quickly turned my head so that no one would see.

Steve continued, "This is what I meant when I said that I now understand my emotions. My whole life, I drank to make the pain go away instead of facing it and working through it. I realized that, if I started drinking again, that I would lose that special person forever. The Universe has a plan for me. I may not understand what it is, but I trust the process. I still have that person in my life and maybe one day we can be more than friends."

David and JoAnn just sat there quietly, while I quickly pulled myself together and thanked them for giving this program a chance.

"We will meet again on Thursday. I hope you both come back because you want to rather than someone asking you to. See you then."

The door shut, and Steve looked at me. "Congratulations. You did a great job."

"*Me?* It was your openness that really connected with those two. At first, I thought we were dead in the water, but you really got through to them."

"I hope I didn't embarrass you. I wasn't expecting to share my painting, but I knew that if I was not vulnerable, they wouldn't open up."

"You took me by surprise, but I appreciate your honesty, and I am glad that you consider me a special friend."

"Just know that if it doesn't work out with Denver guy, I am always here as a friend or more."

"Thank you."

***

That night, I called Hendrix and gave him an update on how the program went.

"Evie, that is fantastic. How do you feel?"

"I feel lucky that they trust me to help these kids. Both have some genuine issues they are trying to manage. I know I can't solve them, but I hope that what they learn through the program will at least allow them to recognize their triggers and be thoughtful about what they do next."

"You were meant to do this. Congratulations."

"So, how was your day?"

"Amazing. I have Aja with me. She helped me cook dinner and now we are working on a puzzle."

"Oh, that sounds like an exciting evening."

"My goal is to take her mind off her mom. She hasn't been doing well for the past few days, so today is all about fun for my little girl."

"I know you love spoiling her, so I won't keep you long."

"Thanks, beautiful. I will call you tomorrow. I love you."

"Love you, too!"

Before I went to bed, I sent Aja and her mother some healing energy. To raise my energy, I remembered when Aja and Hendrix picked me up at the airport in Denver. Her cute sign and magical hug had put a huge smile on my face. I felt my body fill with light energy, my torso tightened, and I focused that energy on Aja and her mother. As the energy transferred, my body relaxed and I fell asleep.

***

Session two of the Something-Something Painting Program went even better than the first. Both JoAnn and David came back, and Steve worked with JoAnn to understand the emotions behind her painting. I continued to work with David to get him to open up.

"I took a look at your painting and didn't know if it was complete or if you wanted to add some more," I told him.

"It's done," he replied.

The only thing that David had put on the canvas was a small, black dot.

"I get a feeling of finality from your painting. May I ask what the black dot represents for you?"

"Stuck, insignificance, end, same thing over and over again."

"Wow. That is very poignant. How did you feel when you painted it? Did it release anything for you?"

"I don't know."

"So, is this emotion from one experience for you, or are these emotions ongoing?"

"Ongoing."

"Can you separate those emotions? You mentioned insignificant. Can you go deeper into that or any of the other emotions?"

David simply shrugged.

"Please trust yourself and open up. Wait—let me show you something first." I pulled out my phone, went to my website, and found the piece entitled "*Me*." "I painted this piece when I first moved to the island. I was going through so much stuff—pent-up emotions that stemmed from family issues. Those emotions ruled my life and how I lived it. Once I trusted myself and was willing to feel the pain, I let it loose, and this was the result. It was a hot mess, but so was I at the time. After I painted that, I cried. The door was open, and there was no going back. But I didn't want to.

"Continually stuffing my emotions down didn't help. I wanted them to be out and free, and I wanted to be rid of the negativity and start anew. Remember, this is a safe place. If you are angry, just throw paint at the canvas. Paint however you want to express the emotions that you are feeling."

David looked at the painting then back at me. "Geez, you were a mess."

"Yes, I was."

After I walked away, from the corner of my eye, I saw David pick up his paintbrush.

When our time was up, David was still painting. So, as to not interrupt him, I asked Steve to let the front office know we would need some more time. JoAnn headed out, and she actually smiled when she said goodbye. Steve returned, letting me know we would need to lock up in thirty minutes.

"You head out. I'll stay here with David."

"Are you sure? I can hang out, if you want me to."

"No, I'll be fine. Call you later."

"Sounds good."

The click of the door seemed to rouse David from his painting trance. He looked over the easel to make sure that I was still there.

"Hi. How are you doing?"

"Hey."

"I am glad to see that you allowed yourself to open up. How do you feel?"

"Raw."

"Is that better than how you felt before?"

"Different."

"Okay. Would you like to talk about this?" I asked.

"No."

"That's fine. Will I see you next week?"

"Sure." With that, David grabbed his school bag and walked out.

I went over to David's easel to clean up his painting area. When I saw his painting, my jaw dropped.

David was brilliant. His painting was filled with pain and fear that he conveyed so clearly. I stared at it for a few moments longer. Then, when I heard the custodian coming down the hall, I put the painting in our assigned closet and locked the door.

Walking out of the school, I noticed David heading down the road in the opposite direction. A nagging feeling told me that he shouldn't be alone at this time, so I jumped into my car and pulled up beside him.

"Hey, you need a ride?"

"Yeah, I guess." David got into the car but didn't look at me.

"Where can I take you?"

"I'm just heading down the road to the market. I have to be at work in an hour."

I gave David a concerned look. "Have you eaten yet?"

"No, I usually grab something from the market."

"How do you like your job?"

"It's a job," David said, still staring out the window. "Trying to help my mom out."

"Cool. I wanted to let you know you are very talented."

He turned toward me. "What do you mean, *talented*? I put my emotions on the canvas like you asked."

"Yes, and what you created was utterly amazing."

David looked at me with fear in his eyes. "You're not going to show that to anyone, are you?"

"No, of course not. This is your work, and you can do with it as you please."

I pulled into the market parking lot and parked the car. "David, before you go, I am curious. In our next session, would you like to continue painting or meet with Steve?"

"Paint," he blurted out. "Um ... If that's okay."

"Yes, it's definitely okay."

Driving out of the market, I continued in the same direction so that David wouldn't know that I had gone out of my way to pick him up. On the ride up island, I called Steve to check in.

"So, how did it go with JoAnn?"

"She is confused and scared. Her home life was terrible. She is happy to be with her foster family but feels guilty that she likes them and is scared that she will be sent back. All she knew was yelling, negativity, and violence at home and does not know how to process her emotions. If you are mad, you lash out—simple. We are developing a good rapport, so I believe I can help her understand that the home life issues were not her fault."

"That is wonderful. I am so glad that she has opened up to you."

"She definitely has trust issues, but she said that she liked me because I was gutsy enough to share that it was you who I liked and admitted it in front of everyone."

"Oh, she is also very perceptive."

Steve laughed. "Yes, she is. How did it go with David?"

"His painting was amazing. Like, crazy good. He doesn't know how talented he is. There was a lot of emotion in it.

Afterward, I gave him a ride to work. He said that he works to help his mother out."

"Hmm ... Is he ready to talk?"

"Not yet. He wants to continue to paint. I think there is a lot more in there that he wants to get out."

"We are making progress."

I smiled. "Yes, we are."

***

When I got home, there was a bouquet at the door. The fragrance of the lilies was heavenly. A note attached to them said:

> *Beautiful,*
> *I am so proud of you. Keep shining your light.*
> *Love,*
> *Hendrix.*

Mmm ... I love that man.

After I got into the house, put my stuff down, and showered, I called Hendrix.

"Thank you for the amazing surprise."

"Just wanted you to know that I was thinking of you."

"Your timing was perfect. We are really making progress with our two students. It is such an honor to work with them, and incredibly, one is an amazing artist."

"Really?"

"Yes. And he doesn't even know it."

"Well, I also have some good news."

"You do?"

"Yes, I just gave my notice and will officially open the doors to the Passion Hunters Unlimited next month."

"Oh, Hendrix, congratulations!" I squealed. "I am so proud of you, and I love the name. How do you feel?"

"Nervous, but I know this is the right move."

"That's what leaps of faith are about. I am learning that, to grow, we have to keep on taking them. So, does this change anything about you and Aja visiting this summer?"

"Nope. Nothing can keep us from coming out. Aja can't wait."

"Neither can I."

Lying in bed that night, I gave my appreciation for all the love and abundance that I had in my life. The simple, little things brought me joy, unlike before when my vision had been clouded. It was like I had viewed life through dark sunglasses. Everything had been dull. No excitement, no joy or love. Now, feeling the warmth of the sun or watching the waves crash upon the shore could make my entire day. Once I stripped away the *stuff*, just sat with myself, and observed, I could feel the energy all around me.

"Thank you, higher self, for showing me what it means to truly live life."

CHAPTER 9 — STORIES

David and JoAnn were making excellent progress. JoAnn was able to express her emotions and identify her triggers. Giving herself grace and moving forward would need to take more time, but she was developing the tools that she would need to work through her feelings. David had a talent for painting and spent most of his sessions doing such. Each time I would encourage him to think about art school, he shrugged me off.

"Why do you brush off my comments about art school?"

"Because it's not going to happen," he snapped.

"Why would you say that? Are you not interested?"

"I can't go to college." His tone was solemn but strong.

"Who says?"

"Life says."

My confused look begged for more.

"Look, the reason why I was sent to this program in the first place was because '*I am not acting like I used to,*' '*I am failing out of my classes,*' '*I am distant.*' I know people think I am into drugs, or I am depressed, but that's not it. My mom is sick, and I have to take care of her. She can't work, so I need to. So, there is no way that I will be able to go to college."

I softened my voice. "David, thank you for trusting me to share that information."

He turned away from me. "It's not like I don't want to leave this island and go to school, but how can I? My mom isn't getting better, and she has no one else. So, I am stuck here." He stopped and hung his head. "Don't get me wrong; I love my mother, and I want to take care of her, but she has no one else." He stopped. "I just want to be able to live my life."

"And you feel guilty for wanting to live your life?" I asked.

"Yes," he replied softly.

"David, there is nothing wrong with wanting to live your life. And I am sure that is what your mother wants you to do, too. The timing of school and other things may just be different than everyone else's. You have the ability to create the life you desire."

"How?" he asked sullenly.

"By focusing on what you want, declaring that you will do what it takes to make it happen, and being open to *how* it happens. I am going through that right now," I admitted before telling him, "The man that I long to marry found out recently that he has a young daughter. He cannot leave Denver, and I just moved to the island to start a new life as an artist and to be with my granddad. Neither of us can leave, but we are committed to living our lives together. We are focusing on what we want and are trusting the process. If you want to go to college, then declare it will happen and know—truly know—that it will."

"All I have to do is say that I want to go to college, and it will happen?"

"You need to declare exactly what you want, but the challenge is believing in the process. The Universe may have you do things that you never thought you could do. Those things may be hard, you may go in a totally different direction than you ever expected, but in the end, it is preparing you for what you desire. Don't try to make sense of it, because you can't. You just need to believe that it will happen."

I could tell he wanted to believe what I was saying but didn't trust me, or himself, enough to do it.

"David, I know it took a lot of courage to tell me what has been going on. Thank you again for trusting me."

He looked directly into my eyes for the first time. "It felt good telling you. I don't feel like I can share that with many people. All of my 'friends,'" he said with air quotes, "or people who used to be my friends, can only talk about leaving for college and what they are doing for the summer. No one wants to hear about a sick mother and stocking shelves at the market."

"Know that we—Steve and I—are always here if you want to talk."

"Thanks."

On the drive back up island, I shared what I had learned with Steve.

"No wonder his painting was so final. He feels his life has reached a dead end."

"What is so crazy is that he cannot even see how talented he is and that, through his talent, so many doors could open."

"Evie, when you are in the dark, sometimes it is hard to see the light, even when it is right in front of your face. Do you know what he will be doing this summer?"

"I didn't ask."

"Hmm ... Maybe I could get him a job with my construction company. I'm sure that he will earn more money doing that than stocking shelves."

We drove in silence for a while. Then Steve turned to me and said, "Hey, congratulations."

"For what?" I asked.

"You broke down his walls. He trusts you now."

"I don't know if I would go that far, but I do know that he felt relief being able to share his feelings with someone."

"Don't trivialize what you have just accomplished. It takes a lot for guys to share. He has been thrown into the provider role and feels like he has to do it all himself. You can show him that he can get help and that it is not a weakness to ask for it."

"Thank you. I appreciate it. I wonder if the school has a program to help him get his GED. Seems like he has missed too much school to graduate, but that should not stop him from getting his diploma. How is it going with JoAnn?"

"We are having fun. She is a delightful young woman but will need to work through many scars."

"Do you think she will stay in her foster home?"

"Time will tell, but she is learning to appreciate what she has there, which has made their home life a lot better."

"Congratulations all around then. The program is working."

Steve smiled and added, "Just like Bill knew it would."

I walked into the house and noticed Granddad had left me dinner. Nice. He always knew what I needed. He had also left me a brochure for the local museum announcing an exhibit on the tribe with a note.

> *Are you free tomorrow night? Want to go with me?*

***

In the morning, I slipped through the bushes with a couple of muffins.

"Good morning," Granddad said before I even opened the door.

"Good morning. I brought breakfast."

"Great. I just made some coffee."

"Thanks for dinner last night. It was just what the doctor ordered."

"How are the painting sessions going?"

"We are making greater progress than I thought we would. I just had a breakthrough with David, and Steve has made a new friend in JoAnn. She is really opening up and has said that her relationship with her foster family is getting better."

"Well, that is wonderful news. You two are really helping those young people. Who says you have to travel around the world to do humanitarian work? You are following in your family's footsteps right here."

When Granddad said that, I got emotional. I hadn't thought about it, but he was right. I was helping just like my mother and grandfather helped others.

"I am free tonight, so we have a date to go to the museum?"

"Yes, we do. Let's head over around four o'clock, and then we can grab dinner."

"Ooo … A night out. Can't wait."

For the rest of the day, I worked in the studio. My inspiration was the emotion that I had felt when David had finally let his walls down. Taking from his original painting, I started with a small black dot. Instead of it being a symbol of insignificance and being stuck, I chose to have it represent a seed, shoved into the dirt, in the dark, buried with more and more crap put on top of it. But, when the light would finally reach that seed, all of the dirt and stuff had nourished it, so it became stronger. It fought its way through the muck and reached for the light. There it could see what was in front of it. Its roots were strong, allowing it to grow tall and resilient. I saw that for David. He would weather this storm and, in the end, be stronger and more powerful for it.

***

"Wow, you clean up good."

I grinned. "You probably know everyone there, so I had to represent."

When we pulled into the museum, there were lots of cars already in the parking lot. The museum was in a wonderful, old historic building on a hill that looked out over the sound. It was interesting seeing all of the artifacts from years gone by.

Granddad ushered me into the room that housed the exhibit, proudly stating, "This will be a permanent installation at the museum."

Pictures lined the walls of tribal members on whaling ships, a lighthouse keeper, others making and selling pottery from the cliffs, and the annual pageant that told our creation story. Wampum jewelry and belts told our stories. Cranberry rakes and an enormous cauldron to process whale oil. Walking through it filled me with pride.

As we looked at each picture or artifact, Granddad had a story to tell. Strangers lingered around us so that they could hear his stories, as well.

"Kid, this is your history, and these are your people. Always remember."

"Thank you, Granddad, for showing me this. I love getting to know this side of my family."

"After I am long gone, know that, as long as our tribe exists, you have family."

That thought warmed my heart, but it was also a stark reminder that Granddad would not be with me forever.

I pushed that notion out of my head. I needed to enjoy the time that I still had with him.

Just as we were leaving the museum, a woman stopped us.

"Attaquin, so glad you came."

"Thank you for the invitation. Helen, this is my granddaughter, Evie. Evie, this is Helen Wood, the director of the museum."

"So nice to meet you, Evie. Your grandfather speaks of you often."

"Nice to meet you, as well. You have a wonderful museum, and this new exhibit is amazing."

"Well, you need to thank your grandfather for that. He was instrumental in making this happen. He petitioned to have this exhibit permanent and was the person who curated all of the pictures and artifacts."

"Granddad, how come you didn't tell me?"

"Because I wanted it to be a surprise."

"Attaquin, I was hoping to have this hung prior to the exhibit going live, but it just arrived, so we will do it now. Please, both of you follow me."

We followed Helen back to the exhibit. Waiting for us was a young man.

"Hi, Attaquin."

"Bob, nice to see you."

Bob hung a placard outside the door to the exhibit that read:

Curated by Attaquin Brown
Dedicated to Evie Prince

I turned to Granddad and smothered him with a hug. "Thank you."

"Anything for you, kid."

Helen took a picture of Granddad and me standing next to the placard. When I looked at it, I thought, *This is a memory I will cherish forever.*

Walking out, Granddad looked at me. "Happy, kid?"

"More than you know."

"Good. You hungry yet?"

"Of course. Where shall we go? We need to celebrate."

"There is a Thai restaurant that I have never tried. Want to go there?"

"Thai?"

"Yes, taking your lead to open up to new and different things."

"Sounds wonderful to me."

***

The Something-Something Painting Program would be ending, and I needed to give Principal Patrick an update, so I made myself a cup of coffee and sat down in front of the computer.

JoAnn is truly a delightful and intuitive young woman who has opened up and developed a trusting relationship with Steve. They are

> *working through her emotions, identifying triggers, and she is learning how to appreciate her life. She told Steve that home life with her foster family has improved. I would recommend reaching out to the foster family to get their assessment of her behavior since attending this program.*
>
> *David is also progressing. He enjoys painting as an outlet for his emotions and has a real talent. He and I have had short discussions about his feelings, but he isn't willing to share too much yet. Even though David has not engaged in much counseling, I feel the time he spends painting is allowing him to work through his feelings versus keeping them pent up.*
>
> *Overall, we are very proud with how the program is going and feel that we are positively impacting these young people. My hope is that the school would agree to continue this program the next school year.*
>
> *Thank you.*

Being a teenager was hard enough when life was good. Adding all this other muck that JoAnn and David were going through could make it unbearable. How many more young people were hiding or pretending to be someone or something that they were not? I hoped they allowed this program to continue because we could help so many more.

I shot the draft over to Steve to get his input before forwarding it to the principal. He was quick to respond with a thumbs-up and confirmed that David could get a job with his construction company if he was interested.

Today would be our last day of the program and, admittedly, I found myself sad knowing that I would not regularly see David and JoAnn. Steve looked a little solemn himself when he entered the art room.

"Well, it's our last day," I stated the obvious.

"Yup, I know. Kind of wish it didn't have to end. I have really enjoyed my time with these young people. JoAnn is my buddy."

The door to the art room swung open.

"Speak of the devil," Steve announced.

"Hi, Steve. Hey, Evie."

"Wow, you look happy. What's up?" Steve asked.

With an enormous smile, JoAnn announced, "My foster family asked if I wanted to be a member of their family."

"What? Like they are going to adopt you?" I shrieked.

"Yup. It will still take some time, but they want me."

"That is wonderful. Congratulations." Steve jumped up and hugged JoAnn.

"Hey, what's going on in here?" David asked, dodging JoAnn's legs as Steve swung her around.

"My foster family wants to adopt me!" JoAnn screamed out excitedly.

"Nice. That is great news."

I looked at David. "How was your day?"

"Not as good as JoAnn's. I found out that I will not be graduating this year. Because I failed too many of my classes, I don't have enough credits to graduate. But hey, I'm not going anywhere, so …"

"David, you can get your GED, or maybe you can take a class over the summer to make up the credits. Have you talked to your counselor?"

"No. Plus, I have to work this summer; maybe two jobs since the market doesn't pay that well."

"Maybe I can help," Steve chimed in. "I asked my boss at the construction company, and he said that they always need help. Can you swing a hammer?"

"Yeah, I took shop my sophomore year. Wait a minute—you asked him already?"

"Yes, Evie let me know your work situation, so I took the liberty to ask."

David couldn't hide his excitement.

"Good. So, if you're interested, I know it will pay more than the market. Maybe that will give you the time to take a summer class."

He looked at both of us. "Wow, thank you for the help. I really appreciate it."

"David, just remember you don't have to do this all by yourself and it is okay to ask for help. We are always here for you," I assured him.

Steve cleared his throat and looked at JoAnn and David. "I would like to thank both of you."

"Why?" JoAnn asked.

"I know you both thought you were asked to participate in this program to help you manage your emotions, and I hope that it did such. But, having your friendship and working with the two of you gave me a purpose, to get over myself and my issues … to really think before I acted because I had others who counted on me. You helped me more than anything that I could have done for you." Then Steve looked at me. "And Evie, thank you for seeing whatever you saw in me to ask that I join you on this adventure. You truly are a special friend."

David's jaw dropped. "So, *you're* the special friend?"

JoAnn rolled her eyes. "OMG, David, you didn't know?"

We all laughed.

"Since this is our last day, why don't we go out and celebrate?" I suggested.

"Sounds good to me," Steve responded, and JoAnn and David agreed.

Before I closed up the room, I handed David all of his paintings. He had six amazing pieces.

David's face was filled with surprise. "I get to keep them?"

"Of course. I told you that they were yours to do with what you wanted. Do you want them?"

He looked at each one. "Yeah, I do."

"Great. Let's put them in the back of my car, and I will deliver them to your house."

We all got into the car then headed out to my favorite bakery. Nothing better to celebrate our accomplishments than with delicious baked goods.

After the bakery, I drove David home to drop off his painting. His mother was home and asked that I come in for a visit.

"Evie, thank you for working with David. His outlook on life has dramatically changed for the better. He said that he owes it to you."

"Thank you, but he did all the hard work. I believe releasing your emotions through painting always brings clarity."

"Well, it has done wonders for David."

"David is a very talented young man. After this program, I hope he continues to paint. He has a natural talent. And please know that you or he can reach out to me anytime, if there is anything that I can do to help you both."

"Thank you, Evie. David said that you were a kind person and now I see why."

I fist-pumped David as I walked out the door. The smile that he gave me in return made this entire program worth it.

***

Working in the studio, I heard Granddad come up the walkway.

"Come on in."

"You are famous," he announced.

I spun around in my chair. "What do you mean, *famous*?"

He tossed me the local paper. On the front page was the picture of us at the museum, announcing the exhibit.

"*Me*? I would say that *you* are the famous one."

"Read the article."

As I skimmed the article, there was a mention of my artistic accomplishments and the Sunshine Studio. "Well, I guess, if I wanted to slide under the radar, my cover has now been blown."

"This is great local publicity for you. Plus, there are plenty of summer folk who get the paper delivered to them or read it online from all over the world."

"Thank you, Granddad. Having the exhibit dedicated to me was an amazing surprise. Not everyone can say that they have a museum exhibit created for them."

"There was so much that I wanted to give you when you were growing up that I was just unable to. This is but a small token."

"Granddad, you have given me more than you can imagine. Without you guiding me through this time in my life, helping me understand the reasons behind the secrets, I would still be living in the dark. You have opened my eyes and taught me how to listen to the messages that the natural world is always providing. Without you, I don't think that I would ever have learned to love me for me."

Granddad pulled me in for a hug and whispered in my ear, "I was given a second chance with you, and I wanted to make it count. Love ya, kid."

"Love you, too, Granddad."

CHAPTER 10 — TRUST THE PROCESS

Summer is always busy but, for me, this one was out of control. Colbie and the boys were coming out for a week, I would be hosting my first art show at the Sunshine Studio, Reva and Brian planned a visit, and Hendrix would bring Aja out for a week. On top of that, somehow, I was supposed to find time to paint.

To get a jump on the summer and to work around sports camps and etcetera, Colbie and the boys planned their visit the first week of June. Colorado schools started and ended earlier than most schools across the country, so they took advantage of it. We had it all planned out. Granddad would take them fishing at least twice, which would give Colbie and me two days where we could just have girl time. We would do the normal touristy things and of course there needed to be beach time.

"Evie, the boys could hardly contain themselves when I told them about the itinerary for our trip. We also plan to spend a day or two in Boston so we can hopefully catch a ball game. I can't wait to see you."

"I know. We have so much to catch up on. This will be a wonderful visit. Send me your flight and bus information, and I will be waiting at the boat."

"Will do."

I couldn't believe it had been over two years since Colbie and I had worked together, and both of our lives had changed dramatically. Her spiritual coaching and my art were taking us both in directions that we had never thought possible. It would be nice to just have some time with Colbie. She always grounded me and put everything in perspective.

Today was food shopping day. Three extra people in the house, two of which were teenage boys, equaled a lot more food than I was used to buying. Before heading down island, however, I went over to Granddad's to see if he needed anything.

"Granddad, heading down island to go food shopping. Colbie and the boys arrive tomorrow, so I need to stock up. Do you need anything?"

"Coffee, a couple of cans of corn beef hash, and some eggs."

"Sounds like you are planning a nice breakfast. So, that's it?"

"Yup, I will be going down myself in a few days, so that will get me through. Have these boys ever fished before?"

"I don't know."

"Well, you might want to buy some motion sickness pills. I don't want to get them out there, they turn green, and have them both over the side of the boat."

"Good point. I will remind Colbie to pack some for the trip."

***

It seemed like, one day, everyone decided it was summer. Everything was bustling again. I should have headed out earlier, but if I took the back roads, I should be able to avoid some of the traffic.

Three hours, one headache, and three hundred dollars later, I was back up island. How was it that they could deliver alcohol, yet someone hadn't started a grocery delivery service? I laughed thinking that, if this painting thing didn't pay the bills, that was something I could definitely fall back on.

Unloading all the food, for a split-second, I thought that maybe I had bought too much. Then I remembered teenage boys, no fast food, and living up island, and I knew I had bought just enough.

***

Colbie et al were arriving at noon into the hotbed of down island. I needed to get down there early enough to find a three-hour parking space so that we would still have time to grab lunch and walk around town.

I waited with the masses as the passengers unloaded, but I didn't see them anywhere. Then I heard someone call my name, and I looked up at the top of the boat and saw Colbie and the boys waving. Unlike people who lived on the island, who sat near the exit doors for the quickest exodus, they were full-on tourists and were enjoying every moment of being on the ferry.

I waved back and relaxed, knowing I still had time before they would disembark.

"Evie."

"Hey, Colbie. Welcome." We gave each other a huge hug.

"You remember the boys, Jeremy and Matt." Both boys towered over Colbie, and they were only twelve and fourteen years old. Their father had been tall, so they were definitely taking after his side of the family.

They both said hello to me in unison.

"So nice to see you all. Glad you made it in one piece. So, what do you think so far?"

"The view was spectacular. Everything so far has been amazing. We all took the opportunity to ride the entire ferry ride on the top deck. The moisture felt fantastic."

"So, are you hungry? Since we are down island, I thought we could grab some lunch then do a little sightseeing."

"I'm hungry," Matt declared, and Jeremy nodded his head in agreement.

"Evie, please know that you never need to ask if they are hungry. Just assume they are."

"Got it."

For the next few hours, we blended in with the tourists, ate lunch, had ice cream, went shopping, and took pictures. By the time we were done, I thought the trip was finally catching up with them.

"How about we head back up island? We can do more sightseeing another day."

Colbie looked at the boys and agreed.

The ride up island, with the windy roads, could put even the most seasoned traveler to sleep. Within ten minutes, the boys were out and Colbie was fighting it.

"Colbie, just go to sleep. I will wake you when we get to the house."

She gladly accepted the invitation to sleep.

Back in the day, the bumpy road up to the house would have awoken them, but since it had been fixed, thanks to Steve, I had to announce our arrival.

"Wakie, wakie. We are here."

"Evie, I am so sorry that I fell asleep."

"Don't worry; it happens to everyone. So, welcome to my humble abode."

"Wow, this is so cool," Matt announced.

"Yes, I would have to agree. This place is brilliant. And is that the Sunshine Studio?" Colbie asked.

"The one and only."

After we unloaded their bags and got them settled, I took them over to meet Granddad. We had barely made it through the bushes before we heard from inside the house, "Welcome. So glad you all came to visit. Come on in."

The boys looked at each other with expressions of *how did he know*.

I looked over and told them, "Granddad always knows."

Granddad opened the door and ushered us in.

"Granddad, this is Colbie, Matt, and Jeremy."

"Hello, everyone. So, these are the young men who will be fishing with me."

Jeremy and Matt were grinning from ear to ear.

"Have you boys ever fished before?"

"Yes, sir, we have."

"Great. On open ocean?"

"Uh …" They both looked at each other. "No, we do freshwater fishing in our local streams."

"Well then, I will have a lot to teach you. I know Evie and your mother are expecting that we catch at least one dinner while you are here so, after you eat tonight, why don't you come over and I will give you some pointers?"

"Yes, sir," they replied in harmony.

"Oh, and call me Attaquin."

I nudged Colbie. "Did you remember the motion sickness pills?"

"Yes."

"Good, because they will need them."

I then smiled at Granddad. "Thanks, Granddad. I will send them over later."

***

Colbie and I bunked together, and the boys shared the extra bedroom. Granddad had them leaving bright and early in the morning, so there was no sleeping in. They needed to have a good breakfast to take their motion sickness pills. Granddad cut them some slack, though, and didn't leave until seven o'clock. The boys were just finishing breakfast when he knocked on the door.

"Ready?" Granddad asked.

"Unfortunately, the time difference has caught up with them, but they should be fully awake and ready by the time you get down to the water," I said.

"Well, they will need to be. Someone has to row the dinghy."

The boys both looked at each other. I couldn't tell if it was fear or exhaustion.

I handed Granddad a cooler filled with drinks and lunch just in case they made it that long. Colbie gave them both a kiss and told them to mind Attaquin and to have fun.

Granddad smiled at Colbie, and then he announced that they were off.

Once the screen door closed, Colbie and I both let out a chuckle.

"Well, this will be an experience for them both. Granddad will teach them a lot, and it won't just be about fishing."

"Thank you, Evie. They needed this time away from Denver and to have some male bonding."

"Good. While they get theirs, I need some girl time. Grab your coffee and let's go out to the studio."

The day was beautiful, and the sun was shining perfectly through the studio windows that cast a warm yellow hue into the room.

"Evie, your space feels so magical. No wonder you are able to create such amazing art. I feel you all around. The energy is like a big, warm hug."

I showed her the paintings that I planned to include in the showing this summer, and then we pulled up space against the wall, drank our coffee, and just talked. I had always said Colbie just grounded me.

Hours passed and our delightful visit came to an end when we heard Granddad's truck pull into the driveway. We were greeted by Matt and Jeremy holding one fish each. Matt had caught a blue fish, and Jeremey had a striped bass.

"We brought you dinner," Matt announced.

"Wow, nice catch, boys. Attaquin, thank you so much for taking the boys out."

"Not a problem. Once they woke up, they were real naturals. Heading out, they got a little green around the gills, but the food you all packed helped settle things down."

"So, Granddad, you going to teach them how to clean the fish?"

"Don't you want to do that?" Granddad replied with a grin.

"No, don't want to ruin your fun."

"Okay, boys, get back in the truck, and we will go to my house, clean the fish, and deliver your mom and Evie some beautiful fillets for tonight's dinner."

"Will you join us tonight?" I asked him.

"Happy to."

When the boys returned, we got our stuff together and headed to the beach. The boys passed out quickly once they lay down on the sand. Colbie and I took a nice, long walk.

"Evie, this place is just amazing. Everywhere you look, there is beauty. No wonder you wanted to move back."

"I am really learning to appreciate what I have here. It does make it hard to think about living anywhere else."

Walking a little farther, I motioned Colbie to join me in sitting at the water's edge. Looking out to the open ocean, Colbie could tell there was something still eating at me.

"There is more. What is it?" she asked.

"Even though I do love it here, I have the urge to travel. I want to experience more of the world."

"That sounds amazing, and I am sure it will add a new dimension to your paintings. Will Hendrix join you?"

"Time will tell."

"I wouldn't worry about it; the Universe has a plan."

"How do you stay so calm when it comes to the unknown?"

"It is not always easy, but instead of worrying what may or may not happen, I try to stay in the moment and envision a positive outcome. Don't get me wrong; I still worry, but it is a lot less than before. I have experienced enough examples that the Universe has a plan for me and that I am always cared for, so I focus on trusting the process."

"I gave that same advice to a young man in my painting class. It is so easy to say it but can be so scary to do it."

"Yes, the process does not always go in a straight line, and you sometimes feel you are going backward. But every experience builds upon each other to prepare you for what you desire. Remember, ego is always lurking to limit and create fear, but if you can tell ego to piss off and trust your heart, the process becomes less scary."

I stood up and shouted at the top of my lungs, "Ego, piss off! I don't need you now! My heart is in control! I trust the process!"

"Well, that is one way to do it. Nice work."

The rest of the week was a blur. All I really remembered was the large amounts of food that was consumed and bouts of uncontrollable laughter.

"Colbie, thank you for making the trip out here. It was a pleasure to have you and the boys with me."

"You have made a wonderful life for yourself. I am so proud of you. You are finally living life, and that is all we can hope for in our time on this earth. Keep on enjoying."

"Thank you, and you are doing a great job with the boys. They are turning into amazing young men. Enjoy Boston and travel safe back to Denver. Let me know when you get back home."

"Will do."

After a big hug, they all turned and walked onto the boat. I waited until I saw them on the outside deck. They all waved and yelled, "Thank you, Evie. We love you!"

CHAPTER 11 — TWO PEAS IN A POD

It was wonderful having Hendrix and Aja here with me on the island. Granddad welcomed them with open arms.

When Aja met Granddad, she took his hand, and I could see him melt before my eyes. They became inseparable.

We spent wonderful days enjoying what the island had to offer. When I painted, Hendrix worked remotely, and Granddad watched Aja. She caught her first fish with him, and Granddad taught her how to clean and cook it. She was better at it than I had ever been.

Early in the mornings, Granddad would wait on the deck, and Aja would crawl out of bed and join him. He would tell her fishing stories and how the big one got away. Some mornings, I would peek out the window to watch them. Granddad was in pure heaven.

"Aja, did you know that Evie was your age when she caught her first fish?"

"No."

"Yes, I took her out on my boat, just like I did with you. She cast her line, and just like that, she caught a fish."

"Wow. Just like how I did it?"

"Yup, but Evie did not like to clean her fish. I always had to do it for her."

Proudly, Aja said, "I cleaned my own fish."

"Yes, you did. I have a surprise for you."

"What?"

Granddad slipped a small fishing pole and reel from behind the deck chair. "Here, this is for you."

"Really? It's for *me*?"

"Yes, so when you come and visit again, you will have your very own fishing pole."

Aja jumped up and ran straight into our bedroom, announcing that she had her own fishing pole. "Daddy, Evie, Granddad gave me my own fishing pole."

In a groggy voice, Hendrix asked, "Aja, did you say thank you to Attaquin?"

"Whoops." She quickly ran back out on the deck. "Thank you, Granddad, for the fishing pole."

"You are very welcome, Aja."

Halfway into their visit, Hendrix spoke to Aja's mom. Her mother was still experiencing health problems.

"How is she doing?"

"Seems like this week has been hard on her. She misses Aja, and her health has not been great."

"Do you know what is wrong with her?"

"She let it slip the day I picked up Aja that she has been fighting stomach issues."

"What type of stomach issues?"

"She won't say, but when it flares up, it is hard for her to care for Aja. Luckily, her mom is close by and can help."

"Is she investigating this further?"

"Not yet. I have encouraged her to do so, but I think she is scared."

"Understandably so."

"She is very guarded, so all I can do is be there for Aja."

That evening, after dinner, we went to the cliffs and got some ice cream then took a stroll on the beach. We could just see the red, red, white beams of light in the distance. Everything felt perfect. We walked hand in hand, and Aja lagged behind, picking up shells and rocks.

"Daddy, wait up!"

"Come on, sweetheart. We can't bring every shell and rock back to Denver."

In that exact moment, I realized I was having déjà vu. I had lived this wonderful experience before. The dream that I had over two years ago, walking down the beach, hand in hand with a man, and a small child calling to their father was this exact moment. In a funny way, I knew two years ago that I would be here with Hendrix, and I knew about Aja before he did.

A warm smile crossed my face as we sat down on the beach and watched the waves roll in and out. Aja playing in the sand. Everything was perfect. It seemed like time stood still. We were a happy little family.

Aja crawled onto her father's lap, and we watched the sunset. She fell asleep on the short ride home.

After putting Aja to bed, Hendrix and I cozied up out on the deck.

"Evie, I need to ask you a question."

"Yes."

"Would you consider moving back to Denver full-time?" He paused when he saw the expression on my face. "I am sorry to have asked that question. I know it would be just as hard for you to leave the island and your granddad as it would be for me to leave Denver and Aja. Plus, I see the twinkle in your eye when you talk about your desire to see the world."

My heart sank. "We both agreed that we could create a life together, right?"

"Yes, and I still believe that we can, but ..."

"But, what? Don't you want to see the world with me?"

"Yes, I do, but I have Aja to care for now, and I can't imagine being away from her. We were both guided that it would take focus and patience for us to create our life together. Evie, the Universe's timing is different than ours. It doesn't mean that we will not live our lives together; it just means that the time is not now. There are things that we still need to do. Your journey is taking you in a different direction, and my journey is Aja."

My eyes filled with tears.

"Please, do not worry. I know we will be together. I hope you share that belief, as well."

"I do. I really do believe we will be together."

"Good, then do not worry. When the time is right, it will happen. Evie, live your life. For so long, you were living for someone else. Live your life for you and share your light with the world."

I took one deep breath and looked at him with loving eyes. "Hendrix Talisman, I love you."

"I know. And I love you, too, Evie Prince."

Even though there was an underlying sadness between us that we would need to wait before we married, we also had a comfort in knowing that we loved each other and, when it was time, we would be together.

The remainder of their trip was filled with flying horses, ice cream, swimming, and playtime with Granddad. We loved watching Granddad and Aja together. They were two peas in a pod.

***

The drive to the boat was quiet, as we both knew it would be some time before we would see each other in person again. Hendrix had his new business and Aja, and I needed to plan for my first art show in the Sunshine Studio.

I parked the car, and Hendrix grabbed their bags. Aja held my hand as we walked to the boat. The ferry had already docked and cars were unloading. In a few minutes, Hendrix and Aja would be boarding.

I knelt down and gave Aja a huge hug. "Thank you for coming to visit me. Did you have a nice trip?"

"Yes, and I can't wait to come back. Granddad said we would go fishing again."

I stood to say my goodbyes to Hendrix. He looked deeply into my eyes; his own misty. We embraced, and I could feel his energy run throughout my body. I didn't want to let go.

A sharp pain stung my heart as we separated. It was as if he was taking my heart.

He saw my face and stroked my cheek then gave me the sweetest kiss. He lifted Aja into his arms, and we all embraced.

As they turned to board the boat, he looked at me. "Remember, I love you, Evie Prince."

"I love you, too, Hendrix Talisman."

***

Driving back up island was a total blur. When I pulled into the driveway, I saw Granddad.

"You okay, kid?"

"No, but I know this time apart is for the best."

Granddad came over and gave me a big hug.

"Hey, I want to show you something. Do you have time to come over to my place?"

"Sure." I followed Granddad through the bushes.

On his kitchen table was an album. We both took a seat next to each other, and he opened it.

"Kid, I know I showed you the DVD, but I also put this together so that you will always know your family." We slowly went through the pages. Pictures of Granddad as a child with his parents. Pictures of him as a young man, his wedding photo, and pictures of my father throughout the years. In addition, there were pictures of him dressed in his regalia. Granddad was such a handsome man, strong but with a gentle smile. My father had been the spitting image of him when he had been young. There were pictures of him fishing, in meetings, and pictures of my cousins and other tribal members.

"There are too many stories and information to share in one sitting. I thought that, on the nights we have dinners together, instead of watching movies, we can look through the album."

"That sounds wonderful," I told him.

"Hey, I know you're tired, and it has been a long, emotional day. Why don't we have dinner tomorrow night?" Granddad got up and went to the fridge. He pulled out a container of chowder and handed it to me. "Take this. I want to make sure that you eat tonight."

"Thank you." I grabbed the chowder and the photo album then headed back through the bushes.

***

My vacation was over for the time being, and I needed to start planning for my first art show in the Sunshine Studio. Beth gave me a list or art enthusiasts who had attended her showings in the past to send personal invitations. The local newspaper agreed to do a story on me to promote the showing, and I would put the information on my website, as well. Then, of course I would create lawn signs leading up to the event that Steve would help me create.

My inventory of paintings was the largest it had ever been. I had held back on sharing many of these pieces with Tatum, with the expectation that if they did not sell at the show, I would pass them on to her so she could share with her larger international clientele.

I needed someone to cater the show, and I knew just the person. Celeste, former high school classmate, now caterer, would be the cherry on top for my first show in the Sunshine Studio. Her business was going strong, so I cashed in a friend chit, and she was able to squeeze me into her calendar.

How far she and I had come. From working in a T-shirt shop and quitting her full-time job at the bakery to starting her own successful catering business all within a couple of years. She was the one who had given me the idea of having my own studio and hosting my own shows. We had both been on a crazy, wonderful ride, and now we were back together again.

Reva and Brian confirmed that they would attend. Hendrix would try, but Aja's mother was still in bad health, so he couldn't commit yet. Things were coming together, and I was feeling confident that I would have a good turnout.

The final step in all of this preparation was to pick the piece that would be on the invitation and promotional materials. To help me decide, I invited Steve, Granddad, David, and JoAnn to dinner. Afterward, I asked them all to join me in the studio.

"So, the reason I asked you all to come out to the studio is to help me pick the featured painting for my art show."

When I opened the doors to the studio, I had all of my paintings on easels around the room.

"Whoa, this is so cool," JoAnn gasped.

"When did you find the time to do all this painting?" Granddad asked.

"This was my winter project. So much has happened that gave me plenty of inspiration."

"I like that one," David said. He had chosen a piece that I had done after Mr. Frank had passed. It was a mixed media piece that expressed the significant impact he had made on my life.

"That is a good one," Steve agreed.

Granddad chose a piece that I did after he and I had gone quahogging. JoAnn liked a small painting that I had done that captured the joy that I had received after meeting Aja in person.

"Well, I was hoping there would be a resounding winner, but at least you all have narrowed it down for me."

"Why can't you put all of them on your invitation?" JoAnn asked. "It will show the diversity of your work."

"Hmm ... Never thought of that. Yes, I could. Thank you, JoAnn, for the suggestion."

She turned and gave me a big smile.

"With that, it's getting late, and you two need to get home. Thank you for making the trip up island to spend time with us."

"Thank you. It was a lot of fun," JoAnn replied.

"And David, if you want to show your work, I would be happy to make a space for you. Never know what may happen. Steve's cousin, Beth, allowed me to have a few paintings at her holiday show, and I sold one. Just saying ..."

"Uh …" he stammered. "Will people know it is my work?"

"Yes, of course."

"Then I don't know."

"David, your work is amazing. I learned this a long time ago—not everyone will like your art, but you shouldn't paint for others. Paint for yourself, and you will always be happy. Just think about it."

"Okay, I'll think about it."

Steve announced, "All right, Steve's taxi is leaving. Gotta get you kids back home. Goodnight. Evie, thanks for a great dinner and, as always, Attaquin, it was a pleasure."

"Thanks," both JoAnn and David said in unison.

Granddad and I watched as Steve drove down the road.

"Those are good kids."

"Yes, they are. They have come a long way."

Granddad nudged me. "So have you."

***

In an effort to clean the house, I begrudgingly went through my enormous stack of mail. *How did I miss this?* It was a large white envelope from Tatum. To my surprise, it was a copy of the *Best Bali* tourism magazine with my interview. She had put a sticky note on the interview page.

Wow, look at me. It was weird seeing a picture of myself in a glossy magazine. I would admit, though, that I liked the picture, but how crazy was it to have people actually want to know about me as an artist?

The picture of the painting leapt off the page. I must have stared at it for five minutes before I read the article, which was good, and they hadn't taken my answers out of context.

A sense of pride came over me. *I'm doing it. Thank you, higher self, for your guidance on this journey, and I look forward to what comes next.*

Tatum had left me a note with the web address for the online article that I could include on my website and to share with family and friends. Knowing that Granddad would not visit a website, I went through the bushes so he could see the article firsthand.

"What's up, kid?"

"Hey, Granddad. I wanted to show you something." I handed him the magazine.

"What's this?" He flipped to the page with the sticky note. "Well, look at that. My granddaughter is famous. Well done, kid."

"Thank you. I was surprised by how well it turned out."

"I'm sure this will get you a lot of attention."

"When I was being interviewed, I put it out in the Universe that I looked forward to seeing the painting in person."

"In Bali?"

"Yup."

"Good on ya. That's how you do it. Can I have a copy so that I can show it around to the boys."

"Sure. I will stop over to the library and make one."

Granddad came over and gave me a hug. "Remember, there is so much more out there for you to see and experience. Enjoy it."

"Granddad, my life is completely different from what it was two years ago. Life is so good—doing what I love, finding love, and who knows what other wonderful things may happen. I know the question may sound crazy, but can someone have too much good in their life?"

"Too much good?"

"What I mean is, haven't I gotten my share?"

"Evie, there is enough of everything for everybody. There is no scorecard or big pie that measures how much good you can have in your life in comparison to someone else. You are deserving of everything wonderful and good. If you start thinking otherwise, then you are closing down, and you will speak that fear into reality."

"Understood. I have never been this happy, and I want it to last forever."

"It is up to you to make that happen."

When I was heading over to the library, I could feel my phone vibrate. *Who could that be?*

"Hello?"

"Evie, it's Triniti."

"Triniti? Are you on the island?"

"No, but I was reading the local island paper and saw the article that they did on you and your upcoming show. I am so proud of you. Congratulations!"

"Thank you. I wish you were here to see it."

"I will be back later this summer, and I will be sure to give you a call so we can hang out."

"That would be wonderful. So, how are you doing?"

"I am happy to announce that I have found myself a co-op artist studio, and I have been selling my pottery."

"That is amazing news. Congratulations! Do you have a website so I can see what you are up to?"

"We are working on that now, but when it is done, I will forward the link."

"Don't forget my offer still stands on introducing you to my agent. If for nothing else than to provide some guidance."

"I haven't forgotten. I am keeping that in my back pocket, and when I am ready, I will cash in the chit."

"Sounds good."

"Best of luck, and see you this summer."

Now, that was an amazing surprise. I hadn't heard from Triniti since last summer. It was wonderful to hear that she was doing well and creating the life she desired.

Walking into the library, I was all smiles.

"What are you all smiles about?" Barbra asked.

"Life is good, and it keeps on getting better."

"Do tell."

"Well, my work has been published in a tourism magazine in Bali, and the local article on my upcoming show was seen by a friend out in Denver."

"That is random. How did she see it?"

"Actually, she grew up on the island, and we met in Colorado. I helped her out a bit, and we caught up last summer when she came home to visit. So, she gets the paper to keep up on what is happening at home."

"That is fantastic. Can never have too much good in your life."

"Funny, that is what Granddad just said to me," I thought out loud.

"Huh? What did you say?"

"Uh … It's nothing. Can I use your copier so I can make a copy of the article for Granddad?"

"Sure. It's back in the office."

Walking out, I slid a copy of the article over to Barbra for her to read. "Thanks for letting me use the copier."

"What? No movies?"

"Not today. See you next week."

CHAPTER 12 — SUNSHINE STUDIO

At three o'clock, the doors to the Sunshine Studio opened for my first showing. Celeste and team were already in the kitchen, getting everything set. Reva and Brian had been helping me set up the room and would serve as my goffers. Granddad was the greeter, and Steve had volunteered to be the bartender—non-alcoholic drinks only. The room looked amazing. To see my art arranged throughout the studio was a dream come true.

Just before guests started to arrive, I ran inside and changed my clothes. Simple summer dress, hair up in a high bun, minimal makeup. I didn't want to fuss too much. Plus, I would be running around, and I wanted to be comfortable.

My team was all assembled, and I hugged each and every one of them as I walked through.

"Everything looks wonderful, Evie. I am so proud of you," Reva gushed.

"Thank you. Couldn't have done it without you all."

"Hey, we were here when you broke ground and hammered the first nail on the studio, so we had to be here for the first show," Brian chimed in.

I stood at the door of the studio with Granddad, taking it all in.

"Kid, you should be proud of yourself. I know your grandparents, mother, and father are all smiling right now."

"Thanks, Granddad. You helped to make this all possible."

"All I did was give you my love."

"And that means everything to me."

The first car pulled into the road, and my heart skipped a beat. It was Steve's cousin, Beth, and she had a car full of friends.

"Beth, so good to see you."

"Hi, Evie. I would like you to meet a few of my art friends, Joe, Frida, and Anthony. Everyone, this is Evie."

"So very nice to meet you all. Please, come on in."

"Evie, the studio looks amazing and your art … so many pieces. You have been busy," Beth commented.

"Thank you. And yes, I have. Please, take a look around and let me know if I can answer any questions."

There was a consistent stream of cars and people coming in and out. I was on my A game, smiling and explaining the inspirations for each of the paintings. The room was full, and then I saw David walk in with his painting in hand.

"I thought about what you said and talked it over with my mom. She agreed with you that I should give it a try."

"David, I am so honored that you are willing to let me show your first piece. I have a space right here for it. Do you have a price in mind?"

"No."

"Well, you need to think about it. I don't doubt that someone will want to buy it."

The room continued to buzz, and I had buyers for a number of the paintings.

Just as I was about to walk outside to get some fresh air, I felt a tap on my shoulder. "Excuse me. Are you the artist?"

When I turned to answer, all I saw was his smile. Hendrix's amazing smile.

"What? You came? How did you …?" My words were jumbled. I wasn't thinking straight. Then I threw my arms around his neck and gave him a big kiss. "Thank you for coming," I whispered.

"How could I miss your first art show? How is it going?"

"Well, I have sold a few paintings already."

"Of course you have," Hendrix replied proudly, looking at me with adoring eyes.

"Hey, I need to introduce you to Reva and Brian."

"What? I finally get to meet Reva?" Hendrix said in an overly dramatic, sarcastic voice.

"Hey, be nice." I grabbed his arm and led him through the room over toward Reva and Brian.

"Reva and—"

"Is this the one and only Hendrix?" Reva's eyes got big as she interrupted me.

"Yes, Reva, this is Hendrix. And Hendrix, this is Brian."

Brian shook Hendrix's hand. "Nice to finally meet the man. We were wondering if you were real," Brian teased.

"You know, she has been keeping you under wraps for a long time," Reva added.

"All right you two," I scolded.

Hendrix looked at me and laughed. "Tough crowd."

Reva took Hendrix's hand. "Sincerely, it is nice to finally meet you. I was wondering who this special person could be to win her heart."

"Or lucky man," Steve chimed in.

My face flushed, and I stammered, "Hendrix, please meet Steve."

Hendrix smiled. "Nice to meet you, Steve. I have heard so much about you. Thank you for supporting Evie. She speaks very highly of you."

"It has been my pleasure. She is a very special woman."

Granddad walked up just in time to break the awkwardness.

"Hendrix, so glad you could make it."

"Attaquin, thank you for keeping my secret."

"Hey, wait. Granddad, you knew?"

Granddad grinned. "Hey, kid, you better get back to your guests. I see someone looking at David's painting."

I looked over to see a couple discussing the painting.

As I approached, the woman asked, "Is this your work? It is very different from the other pieces."

"Actually, no. This young man painted the piece. It is his first shown work." I motioned to David to come over.

"Yeah, hi."

"Young man, this is a wonderful piece. My wife and I really feel the emotion from it. Can you tell me more about it?"

"Uh … uh … Well, it was my attempt to clear my head of some emotions that I had been feeling."

"Yes, I can feel the rawness. I noticed there isn't a price. We are very interested."

"Gee … I don't know."

"Well, how does three fifty sound?"

"Three fifty?" David questioned.

I looked at him and mouthed, *"Three hundred and fifty dollars."*

David looked back at me, trying to hide his surprise. I smiled at him and nodded.

"Sure, that will work."

"Great. I look forward to seeing what else you will create."

"David, why don't you walk them over to Granddad, and he will process the payment."

"Oh, okay." He then looked back at me and mouthed, *"Thank you!"*

I looked over to Steve, and his face was one of a proud father. He gave me a thumbs-up.

The show lasted for another hour, and after all the guests had left, it was only my team that remained.

"Evie, you put on a fantastic show."

"Celeste, remember, you were the one who planted the seed over a year ago. Now look at us. Everyone loved your food. Thank you for helping me out."

"That's what friends do, right?"

"Right!"

I turned toward everyone else. "Thank you all for your support. I couldn't have asked for a better group of friends or a better night."

"And your protégée even sold his painting," Steve added.

"As my agent always says, I am just the facilitator. He did all the hard work."

"Well, we better call it a night," Reva stated. "We are driving back down island, and I still can't figure out these roads."

"Okay, call me in the morning. We will meet you for breakfast or brunch," I replied.

We hugged, and then I gave them directions one last time.

Celeste packed away the last of her setup, hugged me, and was off. Steve said his goodbyes and walked Granddad home before heading out. Hendrix and I pulled up some floor in the studio and relived the evening.

"Thank you for making the trip out. I know it was hard to get away."

"I am committed to us, Evie. I wanted to share this experience with you. And don't worry; Aja is fine. Just know that I won't always be able to make the trip, but I will do everything in my power to make most."

"And I will do the same. Patience and focus, that's how it will work."

"I hope you are proud of yourself. You have truly built an amazing life."

"Funny you should say that. The other day, I asked Granddad if I had too much good in my life."

"Did he yell at you?"

"Almost. You are a big component of this amazing life. Thank you for loving me."

"It is my pleasure. You have brought such light into my life. I knew you were special when I met you all those years ago, but I didn't think I was good enough to win your heart. The person I was back then would never have thought I would be here now."

"For you to not think you were good enough boggles my mind. You are the most loving, insightful, and generous person I know."

"We were both in dark places back then, but now we have done the inner work to realize we are all worthy of joy and love. Thank you for sharing your joy and love with me."

***

The next morning, we met up with Reva and Brian for brunch. Brian and Hendrix hit it off swimmingly, which gave Reva and I a chance for girl chat.

"You are still glowing from last night. How does it feel to have a successful showing?"

"It felt ... natural. Don't get me wrong; there was a lot of prep, but once I was in it, I was very comfortable."

"You looked great, and your guests really gravitated toward you."

Reva flagged down the waiter. "May I have a cup of mint tea?"

"Of course."

"You okay?" I asked.

"My stomach has been queasy. I threw up again this morning."

"I hope it wasn't the food. Hey, what do you mean, *again*?"

"I'm sure it wasn't the food. I have been feeling this way for the past week. Just can't seem to shake it."

Looking at Reva, I noticed her rosy cheeks. "I can't believe I didn't see this before. Normally, I would say that it's love, but I think it is something else."

"What?"

"You're pregnant."

"Huh? No!"

"Why not?"

"Because I didn't think I could."

"Are you late?"

"I don't know. I haven't really thought about it." She grabbed her phone and checked the calendar. Counting the days, she looked at me then whispered, "I am late."

We instantly both started crying.

Hendrix and Brian looked over at us.

"Reva, you okay?" Brian asked.

We both gave reassuring smiles, and they went back to their conversation.

"Do you think I am?"

"I do."

"OMG, what do I do?"

"Get a test, don't drink any alcohol, and call me as soon as you know."

"I didn't think this could happen."

"Are you happy?"

"Cautiously so. When I know that I am for sure, I will be."

"Well, let me be the first to congratulate you, Momma."

"Thank you, Evie. Thank you for being my friend, sister, confidant, and hopefully my baby's auntie."

The remainder of the brunch, we had cheesy smiles on our faces.

Brian looked at us then turned toward Hendrix. "They are up to something."

"Whatever it is, I am sure it is good," Hendrix replied.

***

"Hello?"

"Hi, Tatum. How are you?"

"Evie, so good to hear from you. Are you calling to tell me you have more paintings for me to sell?"

"Well, actually, I do have a few. I will send the pictures with all the details this afternoon."

"Wonderful. Do you know you have uncanny timing?"

"What do you mean?"

"First, did you get the copy of the interview from *Best Bali tourism* magazine that I sent?"

"Yes, I did. It looked really good."

"Yes, I thought so, as well, and it is getting a lot of attention. Mr. Pratama would like to invite you to Bali for a media tour."

"A what?"

"A media tour."

"Really? Are you serious?"

"Yes, I am very serious."

"That if fantastic! OMG, I can't believe this. I am going to Bali! I said I wanted to see the painting in person, and now it is happening." Under my breath, I said, "Thank you, thank you, thank you." Then I asked louder, "When does he want to do the tour?"

"Well, he feels that it would be best if you could be out there within a month to capitalize off of the magazine article."

"How long would I be there for?"

"Just about a week. Can you manage that?"

"I need to make sure my passport is still good; otherwise, it shouldn't be a problem."

"Good. I will get back to Mr. Pratama's team and get all the details. Stay tuned."

After we hung up, I sat there in complete amazement. Bali had always been a place that I had wanted to visit. The scenery, the people, the ocean, the colors, everything just seemed so enchanting, and now I was going.

Oh, I have to call Hendrix.

"Hey, beautiful, what's up?"

"I have been asked to go to Bali to do a media tour. The article in the Bali tourism magazine received a lot of attention, and the hotel owner wants to capitalize off of that and do a press tour."

"Oh, Evie, that is fantastic news. How do you feel knowing that you manifested this opportunity?"

"I did create this, didn't I?"

"Yes, you did. I am so proud of you. When do you head out?"

"Not sure yet, but he wants to do it within the next month."

"For how long?"

"A week."

"Congratulations! Enjoy what you have created and bring us back a souvenir."

"Wish you could come with me."

"This is all you. I am sure you will be very busy. We will go there together, I promise. Maybe for our honeymoon?"

The thought of Hendrix and I going on our honeymoon to Bali filled me with love.

"That sounds perfect."

CHAPTER 13 — CARED FOR

After thirty-five hours of flying, I finally arrived at the Denpasar International Airport in Bali. As the glass doors slid open for me to exit, I was immediately hit with humidity, making it hard to take a breath, and the vibrancy of the colors caused me to dart my eyes everywhere. Blues like I had never seen before. The multicolored architecture and the warm faces of the Balinese people erased the long hours on the plane and filled me with excitement for what was to come. My gaping mouth must have been a dead giveaway that this was my first trip to Bali.

Outside of the airport were multiple people holding signs with names of passengers. As I scanned them, a young man with a gorgeous smile lifted his sign as if to ask, *Is this you?* I looked at the sign and, to my pleasant surprise, it said, "*Evie Prince.*" I smiled, pointed at myself, and nodded.

"Welcome, Ms. Prince. My name is Wayan." I soon learned that Wayan was a common name, thus one that I would not forget.

"Hello."

"Please, may I take your bags?"

I slid my roller bag over to him, and then he gestured for my backpack, but I shook my head.

"Please, follow me."

Wayan took me to a hotel car. He helped me in then puts my bag in the trunk.

"I will take you to the hotel now. It should take us just a few minutes."

The scenery was spectacular. Again, the vibrancy of the colors was awe-inspiring. Granted, I lived on a beautiful island, but these colors ... they were just at a completely different level of intensity.

True to his word, Wayan slowly pulled onto a cobbled, stone driveway. The hotel entry seemed to blend into the scenery. The wood, glass, and marble were magnificent accents to the blue-green water and the swaying palm trees.

Wayan collected my bag and escorted me into the hotel. There was a faint smell of gardenia in the air that put me in a peaceful state.

"Ms. Prince, please." Wayan motioned for me to take a seat while he checked me in.

When he came back, he told me, "Mr. Pratama would like to meet with you in a few hours for dinner. Please meet him here, in the lobby, by six o'clock. You will join him at his newest hotel to view your painting and have dinner."

"Thank you, Wayan. Your hospitality is impeccable."

Wayan bowed his head. "I will be your driver during your stay here in Bali. If you need anything, please ring down to the front desk and they, or I, will assist you."

A young woman from the front desk came over to me, key in hand, and then she escorted me to my room.

Down a short hallway was a beautifully ornate door. She unlocked it then allowed me to walk through first.

OMG, this is spectacular, I said to myself, or I hoped I said it to myself. By her smile, I figured I had actually said it out loud.

After she gave me a tour of the suite, she smiled as she closed the door.

When I knew she had walked far enough away, I squealed and jumped up and down like a little trick dog. I couldn't believe that this was where I would be staying. Everything was so perfect that I almost didn't want to touch a thing, and the pool right off of the bedroom was the icing on the cake. *What!* This was amazing. I took a photo of every inch of the suite so that I could send it back to Hendrix and Granddad.

Once I calmed down, unpacked my things, and took a quick shower, I went outside to just *be* in the moment. Sitting with the sun on my face grounded me instantly, allowing me to slip quickly into meditation.

"*Evie, feel and enjoy*," played over and over in my head.

***

At six o'clock sharp, I was in the lobby, where I noticed Wayan standing in front of the hotel car. He then opened the door for a well-dressed, middle-aged man who rushed toward me.

"Ms. Prince, so very nice to meet you. I am Wayan Pratama."

"Mr. Pratama, it is wonderful to meet you, and thank you for the opportunity to visit your beautiful island. Please, call me Evie."

"It is my pleasure. Your talent has put many eyes on my newest hotel, and I appreciate that. Please, let me take you to dinner," Mr. Pratama said as he started to guide me toward the car.

"I own several hotels in Bali and throughout Indonesia," Mr. Pratama explained on the way to his newest hotel. "The hotel you are staying in is my favorite. I wanted to give you the real Bali experience. My newest hotel is a bit different. As you will see, it is very modern and is in a more populated area. The audience for this new property is younger and single versus family or honeymooners.

"Your painting has caused such a stir with the guests that their desire to share everything on social media has provided much more publicity than I could have ever hoped for."

"That is wonderful! I am so pleased that your guests have enjoyed the piece."

We drove a few more minutes, and I could feel the energy of the area change. There was definitely a different vibe to this section of Bali. The pace seemed to quicken. People were everywhere. The lights, traffic, and the sounds of the city filled me with anticipation.

Wayan slowed, pulling the car up to the front of the hotel, where an older woman with the most piercing green eyes greeted us.

"Mr. Pratama, your table is waiting."

"Thank you, Ni Putu. Please meet Evie Prince."

"Ms. Prince, it is nice to meet you. I have your itinerary for the rest of your stay."

"Oh, wow. Thank you."

"Don't worry about that now, Evie. We will have a wonderful dinner, then Ni Putu will join us again and run through the press tour with us both."

As we walked through the lobby, Mr. Pratama stopped and pointed to my painting.

I looked up and gasped. Seeing it in its home gave the painting a new energy. I still saw the emotion, but it somehow looked different.

Mr. Pratama laughed when he heard my gasp. "That has been the reaction of everyone who looks at this painting."

"Well, it definitely looks different here than it did back home in my studio," I admitted.

***

Dinner was exquisite. We had multiple small plates filled with skewered spiced meat—babi guling, or roasted pork; lawar, a meat, vegetable, and coconut dish; and urab, a traditional vegetable salad. For dessert, we had laklak, a rice flour and coconut milk pancake served with sugar, grated coconut, and ice cream.

"Mr. Pratama, dinner was delicious. Thank you."

"Of course. I am so glad you enjoy our traditional foods."

Moments later, Ni Putu joined us.

"Mr. Pratama and Ms. Prince, the next few days will be very busy. You have interviews with several art magazines, the local newspaper, one radio interview, and a television morning program. Unfortunately, Ms. Prince, I could only get you an afternoon and evening free to sightsee."

"Thank you. I appreciate the time. I understand the importance of these interviews, and I know this will not be my last visit to Bali."

Ni Putu handed me a large envelope. "All the information you will need to prepare for the next few days is in here. Please be in the lobby by the scheduled time, and Wayan will drive you to each of your appointments. He is also a wonderful tour guide, so I am sure he will show you the sights, if time permits."

"Thank you, Ni Putu, and thank you, Evie, for your willingness to join me on this press tour."

"Honestly, this is the most exciting thing that I have ever done. It is my pleasure."

Ni Putu smiled. "One last thing, Ms. Prince; Ni Kadek and Nyoman from the *Best Bali* magazine would like to show you around on your free day. If you are interested, I will confirm that with them and arrange for your pickup."

"Oh, yes, that would be wonderful. Thank you."

After a long day and a half of travel, an evening of amazing food and scenery, I was ready to sleep. Back in my room, I sent both Hendrix and Granddad a text telling them about my day and shared some photos. Even though I wanted to enjoy my suite more, all I could do was to change my clothes, wash up, and get in the bed that seemed like a cloud draped in sheer curtains. I happily floated off to sleep.

***

Beep, beep, beep, beep. Beep, beep, beep, beep.

I woke with a start. Looking around, not really processing where I was. I hit the clock next to the bed, but it didn't stop the beeping noise. Then I sat up and realized it was the phone.

"Hello?" I slowly croaked out.

"Ms. Prince, this is your seven o'clock wakeup call. It will be twenty-eight degrees Celsius, or eighty-two degrees Fahrenheit. Have a pleasant day."

"Oh, oh, thank you."

I hung up the phone and lay back down. *No, Evie, get up.* The bed was a trap. A luxuriously comfortable trap.

After a brief meditation outside and a shower, I got dressed in a simple, colorful dress and a light scarf. If Bali was like the United States, it seemed like we always kept our air-conditioning up so high that you would freeze inside. *Huh*, I wonder if they even used air-conditioning since everything was so open. Oh well, I brought the scarf just in case.

Placing the itinerary envelope in my backpack, I then headed to the restaurant for breakfast.

"Good morning, Ms. Prince. May I bring you breakfast?"

Everyone was so cordial and accommodating.

"Yes, thank you."

The young woman turned and walked away. A few minutes later, she returned with a tray of coffee, juice, and nasi goreng, which was the Balinese version of fried rice with fresh vegetables. Not what I was used to for breakfast, but it looked and smelled amazing.

As I enjoyed my breakfast, I took out the packet of information that Ni Putu had given me. Today was a busy one. A radio and two magazine interviews. Wow, she even had sample questions for me. Nothing seemed to out of the ordinary, so I felt comfortable with the day.

I was so busy eating and going through the interview information that I hadn't even tried my coffee yet. It smelled different. When I took a sip, it was almost as magical as Hendrix's coffee. *Yum*. This could really become a habit.

I finished just in time to meet Wayan out front of the hotel. He was waiting by the car for me.

"Good morning, Ms. Prince."

"Good morning, Wayan. And please, call me Evie."

He slowly pulled away from the hotel and told me that we had a little bit of a longer ride this morning. "How was the hotel and your night's rest?"

"Everything here has been amazing. Even the coffee. Thank you," I complimented.

"Oh, so you like our coffee? I am glad to hear that. We are well known for our coffee. It is very special."

"How so?"

"Our coffee is called kopi luwak. The coffee beans have been digested by an animal called the palm civet then excreted."

"I'm sorry. Did you just say that the bean was eaten then excreted by a small animal?"

"Exactly. Don't worry; it is very safe."

"Oh, okay," I said suspiciously.

As we drove, Wayan pointed out interesting sights, like the Sanur Beach and the Hindu Goa Lawah Temple. Finally, we arrived at our first stop of the day—a local radio station that catered to the twenty-something population. Wayan parked the car then escorted me into the building.

Once inside, I was ushered into the studio, where two young men were seated around a microphone. One was reading a script, while the other looked at me and smiled.

"Welcome back to *Radio Bali*. We are joined this morning by Ms. Evie Prince, artist extraordinaire, whose painting at Bali's newest downtown hotel has received a lot of attention.

"Good morning, Ms. Prince. My name is Wayan."

"And I am Made. Welcome," his partner announced.

"Good morning, and thank you both for having me here today."

"So, let's jump right in. Your piece conveys a lot of emotion; can you tell us what was your inspiration?"

I smiled at the simple question. "I use painting to help me work through my emotions. This painting highlights emotions that had been with me for most of my life that were not helping me. The painting depicts those emotions and ultimately the release and resolution of them."

"Very interesting. I read in the *Best Bali* magazine that you use a special technique. Can you explain that to our listeners?" Made asked.

I chuckled then cleared my throat. "I like to call it the something-something technique. Unlike most, I paint what I feel, not necessarily what I see. I take the emotion and put it on the canvas versus the actual detail of the inspiration for the painting."

"Oh, so that is why I felt so much emotion when I saw your painting," Wayan added.

The rest of the interview went by quickly, and then I was back in the car, heading to the next appointment.

"Ms. Evie, are you pleased with how it went?"

I grinned. "Yes, actually, I am very pleased."

"Are you hungry? We can stop at a roadside stand and grab some nasi goreng."

"Oh, I had that for breakfast."

Wayan smile. "Yes, we eat that often. Sometimes, three times a day."

"Huh. Sure, I'm game."

"Great. I know a wonderful stand."

Within a few minutes, Wayan pulled the car over and jumped out to buy us lunch.

"We can eat at the beach, if you would like."

"Oh, yes, please."

Even though I had the same thing for breakfast, it was equally good for lunch.

The view on the beach was breathtaking. The water was so clear, and the sun was not too hot. It felt so tranquil.

Before getting back in the car, I took a few photos then asked Wayan if he would take a photo with me. He blushed then finally agreed.

"Say, *cheese*."

"Cheese."

The remaining interviews went smoothly, and just like that, the day was over.

"Ms. Evie, we have arrived." Wayan could tell I was tired; maybe because I was dozing off in the back seat.

"Oh, oh, thank you." I tried to sound like I had been awake, but I could tell it didn't work.

"Ms. Evie, may I suggest you order room service tonight? They will set it up by the pool so that you can relax."

"That is an amazing idea. Thank you, Wayan."

"Have a wonderful evening, and I will see you tomorrow."

Taking Wayan's suggestion, when I got back to the room, I ordered room service. Finally, I had a moment to check my phone. Both Hendrix and Granddad had responded to my texts and photos.

Trying to put this experience into words seemed almost impossible. To be honest, I was too tired to try, so all I did was send more photos with a big smiley face and heart emojis.

No sooner than I had put my phone down, my doorbell rang.

"Room service."

I opened the door, and the waiter set my dinner out by the pool. He then smiled and quietly walked out. Yet another amazing dinner of spiced meats, fresh vegetables, and beautiful desserts.

After I let my food digest, I slipped into my swimsuit and waded into the pool. Laying my head back, I let my body float. The clear night was spectacular. Stars, a warm breeze, and the smell of gardenias. I was in my happy place.

Tomorrow was the morning television show with Mr. Pratama, so I cut my pool time short, showered, and went to bed.

***

Wayan and Mr. Pratama were both at the car when I exited the hotel.

"Good morning, Ms. Evie," Wayan greeted.

"Good morning. I am sorry if I kept you waiting," I told Mr. Pratama.

"No, Evie, I needed to pick some paperwork up here, so I asked Wayan to bring me over early. You are right on time. Is everything to your liking?"

"Mr. Pratama, this hotel and the service are heavenly. Thank you."

"Wonderful. So, are you ready to be on television?"

"Ready as I will ever be," I said with a smile, while trying not to freak out.

During the ride, Mr. Pratama gave me a bit more information about the television show, the audience, and what to expect. I knew he was trying to ease my mind, but I got more nervous than I had hoped.

We had twenty minutes before going on air, so I asked to be excused to use the ladies' room. Thankfully, no one else was in there, which allowed me to speak freely to myself.

"Evie, pull yourself together. Remember, you manifested all of this—enjoy it." I looked in the mirror and witnessed firsthand how my face changed when I was anxious. No wonder Hendrix and Tatum were always reminding me to smile.

It was time I got back, so I looked at myself one last time, gave myself a smile, and took a deep breath.

Within half an hour, the interview was over, and we were heading back out to the car.

"So, Mr. Pratama, how did I do?"

"Wonderful, Evie. You did a fantastic job."

I smiled. "Would you tell me otherwise?"

"Yes, Evie, I would. Why do you ask?"

"Because I don't really remember any of it. It felt like I went blank, but I know my mouth was moving and they were nodding their heads, so I guess what I said made sense."

"How interesting. You sounded perfect, and you had a very pleasant smile on your face. Nice job. I will ask the studio to send you a clip for your records."

"Thank you. That would be great."

"Actually, I will get Ni Putu to get you the print articles, radio interviews, and television clip."

After Wayan drove us directly back to my hotel, Mr. Pratama waved goodbye, telling me, "Have a wonderful time sightseeing, and I will see you again tomorrow."

When I got back to my room, I noticed it was only nine o'clock in the morning. I had a few hours before I met Ni Kadek and Nyoman for sightseeing, so I relaxed and lounged in the pool. I couldn't tell if I was tired because of the travel, time difference, or always talking about myself. It all took so much out of me.

Floating, hearing the muffled sounds of the water around my ears, I wondered, *Why is it so easy to be in the moment here?*

"*Because you are relaxed, open, and know that you are cared for.*"

"That is so true. I wish I could feel this same way back at home."

"*You can.*"

"How?"

"*By relaxing, being open, and knowing that you are cared for.*"

"Yes, but I don't live in a hotel and have a driver at home."

"*No, but if you know you are always cared for, life could be as easy. Live in your heart, not in your head.*"

***

With my backpack on and my favorite running shoes, I felt more like myself. I arrived out front with a few minutes to spare before Ni Kadek and Nyoman arrived. Looking around the lobby, I noticed a small gift shop, so I popped in to see if I could grab a few souvenirs.

"You may want to wait until you visit the Ubud market," I heard someone say. When I turned around, I saw Ni Kadek standing there. "Evie?"

"Yes, Ni Kadek, so nice to see you. Thank you for taking the time to show me around. Where is Nyoman?"

"Waiting in the car. We should go, as there is a lot to show you."

"Wonderful."

"Welcome, Evie," Nyoman greeted me as I got in the car. "We have a busy afternoon planned. Are you ready?"

I grinned. "Definitely."

Our first stop was the Tegalalang Rice Terraces. The lush green steps, or terraces, didn't look real. It was as if they were a plush carpet, just waiting to be rested upon. Next was the Monkey Temple. It was everything that people said. We could only walk around the outside, though, as the temple interior was closed to the public. Nevertheless, the monkeys truly stole the show. Everywhere you looked, there they were. I had a wonderful vision of seeing Aja sitting on the ground, playing with a group of monkeys. Close to the Monkey Temple was the Ubud market. Now that was where I did some damage. The colorful fabrics, wood carvings, and rattan bags would all make wonderful gifts and souvenirs. Our last stop of the day was to Taman Ayun Temple. Ni Kadek and Nyoman considered the architecture and temple gardens to be the most attractive in all of Bali. It was an amazing ending to an equally amazing day.

As we approached the hotel entrance, I gave a sigh of relief. Ni Kadek laughed. "Had enough?"

"Yes, I surrender. That was a wonderful whirlwind tour."

"We tried to show you the most popular spots, hoping it will make you want to return," Nyoman admitted.

"Oh, I definitely want to come back. My fiancé and I said that this would make a wonderful honeymoon spot."

"Please let us know if you return. We would love to host you again."

"Thank you both for your hospitality, and please, if you are ever on the East Coast of the United States, let me know so you can visit my island, Martha's Vineyard."

"Oh, we have heard of that island. Thank you."

When I was out of the car, I waved goodbye then slowly walked into the hotel. My backpack was heavier than when I had left, and I was tired, but I had a smile on my face.

Back in my room, I unloaded, showered, ordered room service, and then I went through the many photos of my day. *Wow, what a life I have.*

"And you created it."

***

My last full day in Bali was filled with the remaining magazine interviews with Mr. Pratama. All went well, and I finally felt comfortable with my and the painting's story.

On the ride back to the hotel from the last interview, Mr. Pratama asked, "Would you like to join me for dinner? We have a traditional Balinese dance demonstration that I would love for you to see."

"Yes, that would be fantastic."

"Great. I have some work to do here at the hotel, so I will meet you at the restaurant in an hour."

Dinner, company, and the traditional dance demonstration filled my heart with joy. The beauty of the dance, the flavors, smells, and colors gave me a sensory overload. By the time I fell into bed, I was already asleep.

Then, the next morning, Wayan met me outside of the hotel and loaded my bag into the car.

For as much as I had enjoyed this trip, I did long to get back home. I missed the island, seeing Granddad, and speaking with Hendrix. It was time to go back home.

"I hope you enjoyed your visit."

"Wayan, I did. Thank you for all of your help. It was a trip that I will never forget."

"I hope you will come back."

"I plan to. Actually, I will. I just declared it."

CHAPTER 14 — HOME

A day and a half later, my plane finally landed in Boston. It was late, so I stayed the night then took the first bus back to Woods Hole to catch an early ferry. Greyhound was my new Wayan.

Seeing Granddad waiting for me as I stepped off the ferry filled me with joy. How I missed him.

"Hey, kid, how was your trip?"

"It was amazing. Bali was magical. It was a whirlwind week, but I am happy to be home. I got tired of talking about me all the time. Each interview, they would ask similar questions and expected me to share my life with them. At first, it did not come naturally, but by the end, I will admit I did pretty good."

"Well, it's good to have you back."

The ride home, Granddad started peppering me with questions about the trip.

"So, tell me everything. Would you go back?"

"Definitely. The weather, sights, sounds, food, and people all made me feel welcomed. I didn't think colors could be so vibrant. One afternoon, I was able to connect with the two people who interviewed me for the *Best Bali* tourism magazine. They gave me a wonderful tour and showed me the sights. It was exhilarating but exhausting. I missed home."

"There is nothing wrong with that, Evie. Just because you want to see the world, it doesn't mean that you have to live there. Home is home, and it is your safe place. It is a place that you can always come back to, to recharge the batteries and ground yourself."

"This will always be home to me, Granddad."

He smiled and, under his breath, I heard him say, "Good."

***

After a few days, my jet lag dissipated and life got back to a normal pace. There was so much inspiration from my trip that all I wanted to do was paint temples, monkeys, mountains, hillside terraces, beaches, forests, and the beautiful faces of the people. Vibrant was the word that always came to my mind when I thought back to my visit. Everything was vibrant.

After a full day in the studio, I cleaned up then went into the house to make dinner. Granddad had already been there and had left me a pot of chowder with a note.

Sorry, I can't join you tonight. Have a meeting.

See you in the morning.

How did he always know what I needed?

As the chowder heated, I checked my phone.

Evie, it's Tatum. Please give a call.

I turned off the chowder and called her. I needed to give her a recap of the press tour, so her reaching out was perfect timing.

"Evie, thanks for calling. Welcome back."

"Thanks."

"How was your trip?"

"Amazing. I have always wanted to go there, and I am so happy that I got the chance. The people were so gracious and everything—food, people, sounds, smells, colors—were all so vibrant. It was magical, and the energy was healing."

"I am so glad to hear you say that. You made a great impression on Mr. Pratama, and you both received an enormous amount of press from your visit."

"Really?"

"Yes. Your something-something technique definitely resonated. So much so that Mr. Pratama would like to offer you a residency."

"You mean, like an artist in residence? Like what they do at art museums?"

"Exactly. He feels your art would capture the true essence of Bali."

"Wow. I don't know what to say."

"You don't have to say anything. Think about it."

"How long is the residency?"

"Six weeks. You would live in one of the hotels and food would be provided. He would request that, twice a week, you teach a class to his guests, and he would have first dibs to purchase whatever you paint while in residency."

"Seriously?"

"Amazing, isn't it? I told you that you made an impression."

"Huh? When is he thinking?"

"It would be in the dry season, so April through October."

"So, I have some time."

"Yes, you do. But he would like to know a few months in advance so that he can prepare."

"Understood."

"Can I tell him you are interested?"

"Yes, I am interested."

"Wonderful. Evie, you have the magic touch. Congratulations."

After we hung up, I just sat there in shock until the grumbling of my stomach aroused me from my trance. I went back to the stove and turned the burner back on.

As I stirred, a rush of emotions flooded my head. Anxiety, questions, and excitement bounced back and forth like a table tennis match in my brain. How did this happen? Could I do this? What about Hendrix, the house, Granddad?

I took my bowl of chowder and sat on the couch. The chowder tasted so good that my mind shut down as I savored each bite.

Later that evening, Granddad stopped by, and I gave him the news.

"That is fantastic. Are you going to do it?"

"I would love to, but ..."

"But, what?"

"What about you and the house? I am still teaching the kids at the high school."

"Are you trying to talk yourself out of not taking this opportunity?"

"Why would you say that?"

"First, I am fine. Second, I have been taking care of this house for years; what is six weeks? And finally, you and Steve seem to have a great program going. I am sure that they would be happy for you to take a break."

"You're right. Ego, the fearmonger, has clouded my head. I can do this. I will accept his offer."

"Wonderful, kid. You deserve all of this success and more. You are creating a wonderful life for yourself."

***

When I gave Hendrix the news, he was ecstatic for me but wasn't surprised.

"Evie, remember when I said, *share your light*? This is all part of the Universe's plan for you. Enjoy and know that you will be amazing. Aja and I are here, and we are not going anywhere. We love and are so proud of you."

"Thank you. Your support means the world to me."

"Hey, we are a team, right?"

"Yes, we are a team. It has been a while since I have asked for this, but may I have a hug?"

"Coming at ya."

I closed my eyes and could feel his energy surrounding my body. Warmth and love were all around me. "Thank you."

"My pleasure."

Prior to going to sleep, I meditated on this new opportunity. This was what I had asked for—to see the world, to experience the sights and sounds—and now I was unsure. Granddad was right. Why did I always try to talk myself out of things?

Clear as day, I heard, *"You are scared."*

"You didn't have to be so blunt about it. Yes, I will admit it. I am scared."

"Have you asked yourself why?"

I sat quietly for a few moments. "Because it is different. I don't know what will happen. Wonder if I fail."

"Is that your heart or your ego saying that?"

I thought for a moment. "My ego."

"*Remember, your ego creates limits, and your heart is limitless. Evie, you must continue to take leaps of faith and believe in your own power to continue to grow. You have manifested this opportunity. Now enjoy the ride.*"

When I opened my eyes, I knew I had to trust the process and that everything would work out exactly how it should.

***

My sleep was unsettled. Thinking about the opportunity in Bali elevated my insecurities. An image of me standing on a cliff edge, contemplating stepping off, continually ran through my mind. I knew I had to step off, but no matter how hard I tried to lift my foot, I was unable to. The image remained with me when I awoke.

What is this about? Why would I need to step off of a cliff? Why is my foot stuck?

I needed to change my focus, clear my head, and seek clarity.

Eating breakfast, something caught my eye. The sunlight coming through the window illuminated a spider's web in the bookshelf's corner. Two thoughts crossed my mind. First was that I needed to do a better job cleaning, but second was how amazingly complicated the web was. Inspecting it, I saw the artist herself. I didn't want to disturb her, but I also didn't want a roommate.

Grabbing a piece of mail from the stack, I carefully lifted her and placed her outside. Unfortunately, I destroyed the web, but it would have been removed when I got around to cleaning, anyway.

Before completely wiping it away, I noticed the chakra book that Colbie had given me prior to leaving Denver. *Wow, I haven't looked at this book in forever.* I wiped it off and flipped through the pages. The book fell open on the root chakra. *"An imbalance may cause a feeling of being unsettled, fear, or nightmares"* was the first thing that I read.

Hmm, could my root chakra be blocked?

Reading further, it said physical symptoms might include problems with the lower back, legs, or feet issues.

When I worked with Colbie a while back to manage the issues I had with making my grandparents' room my own, she had given me a recorded root chakra meditation. The meditation had worked wonders, and opening this chakra could only help alleviate my insecurities about the Bali residency.

The beach was a perfect place to do this meditation. Finding a secluded spot, I sat down and put my earbuds in. As it had done in the past, I became completely relaxed and grounded. Her voice was angelic, and I felt at peace.

For the next few days, I continued to listen to the meditation. Each time, I became more grounded and secure.

One afternoon, in the studio, I heard, *"Step off the cliff."*

"Step off the cliff? What are you talking about?"

"Visualize yourself stepping off the cliff."

"But I couldn't do it in my dreams, so why would I be able to visualize it now?"

"Take a deep breath and close your eyes."

Closing my eyes, I could see myself at the cliff. My feet were right up to the edge. I was so close that, if the wind blew, I would fall off. My leg still felt heavy, but now I could lift it. Slowly, I stepped off the cliff, but instead of falling, I found myself walking through a door. A sense of relief and release came over me.

"I did it."

From that point on, my concerns about accepting the residency in Bali slowly went away. Granddad was right; he has been taking care of my house for years. Steve and I could figure something out to allow me to take off time from the Something-Something Painting Program. Hendrix supported me completely and was happy that I had this opportunity.

I can do this.

CHAPTER 15 — THIS AWAITS YOU

The crazy summer was ending, and I longed for the quiet of the fall. My focus for the winter was to paint and spend time in Denver before heading out to Bali for the residency program. They gave Steve and I the green light to continue the Something-Something Painting Program at the high school. It needed a bit more structure to allow additional young people to take part. I committed to the first semester, but I let them know I had an amazing opportunity to paint oversees. So, in my absence, Beth would run the painting portion of the program while I was away. Still so many details to figure out, but at least I had time to actually think.

Oh, and Reva and Brian were pregnant, so I needed to schedule a trip off island to Connecticut to visit them and see Reva's growing belly in person. Huh, it felt like I already had my fall and winter well planned.

After lunch, I wanted to get into the studio and paint, but my higher self had other plans for me. Walking out to the studio, I heard clearly, *"Take a drive around the island."*

"What? Now?"

"Take a drive around the island."

Letting out a deep sigh, I agreed. "Fine." I went back into the house, grabbed my bag, and jumped into the car. "Where am I going?"

"Just drive down the main road."

Knowing that this adventure had a purpose, I settled into the drive, looked around, and enjoyed the scenery. I let my mind wander. The memory of the first time I had heard my higher self filled my head. The thought made me laugh, as I had been sure that I had gone crazy. Now I talked, laughed, and argued with my higher self all the time, as if it were second nature.

At the fork, I was guided to take one of the back roads that I had not traveled all summer. There was a sharp curve in the road that I drove slowly around. You never knew when you would come up on a cyclist or someone walking.

In the middle of the curve, I was told to take a right onto a dirt road that I had never been down before. Fully expecting to run into a gate or something, it surprised me that the road was open. There were no homes on either side that I could see.

Hesitantly, I kept on driving. At the end of the dirt road, I parked the car, needing to see where I was. I walked until I came to a clearing. A magnificent open pasture that had a perfect view of the ocean. Where was I? All I could do was stand there and take in the beauty. I then slowly made my way farther in and sat down in the clearing.

Losing myself in the majesty of my surroundings, I heard, *"This awaits you."*

"What do you mean? I don't understand."

"You will."

On my drive back home, the thought that *this awaits you* kept rolling around in my head. In time, I knew I would receive clarity, but until then, I needed to paint my experience. Green of the pasture, dark blue of the water, light blue and white for the sky, grey and moss green of the weathered boulders. The sensation of limitlessness enveloped me with the wide-open pastures and the vastness of the ocean. Complete freedom.

Painting this experience was liberating. Each stroke provided more and more clarity. I realized I was being shown my future. The only limitation was what I created.

***

Reva and Brian officially announced that they were pregnant, so I had to see the growing belly for myself. Granddad gave me a ride down island to catch the first boat, and then I jumped on a Greyhound bus to Stamford, Connecticut.

Before this life change, I wouldn't have been caught dead traveling by bus, but when you lived on an island, you learned quickly that there were many different and great options for travel.

The bus came to a stop, and the driver loudly announced, "Stamford, Connecticut." Good thing because I had dozed off due to the early start of my day.

I grabbed my duffle then jumped off to see a radiant Reva waiting for me. Immediately, like a bug to a flame, I was drawn to her belly. I didn't even give her a hug. I dropped my bag and started talking to her tummy.

"Uh ... Hello? I'm up here."

"Yeah, yeah, I know, but I wanted to say hello to the baby first."

She laughed. "You are so crazy."

I stood up and gave her an enormous hug. "What do you expect? I am a first-time auntie."

"Hey, hey, you are going to squish the baby."

I released my hold. "Oh, sorry."

"Don't be silly. I was just kidding. How was your trip?"

"Easy-peasy, and I got to take a nap. Having someone else drive is really nice."

"Well, welcome to Stamford, Connecticut."

"We are definitely not in New York anymore."

"No, we are not. Are you hungry? We can grab some lunch since we are out."

"Yes, I am starving. What's good to eat around here?"

"I've had some killer morning sickness, so I have been trying to lighten my diet and eat more healthy things. There is a great Mediterranean spot down the road."

"I'm game."

Once we were seated, all I could do was smile at Reva. She just looked so happy and full of life.

"What's up?" she asked, looking at me strangely.

"You look amazing. Your energy is pure light. How do you feel?"

"Other than throwing up every morning, I'm doing great. It is a crazy feeling knowing that something—I mean, someone—is growing inside of you," she said while rubbing her belly.

"Does the baby respond to the rubbing?"

"Huh?"

"You are rubbing your belly."

Reva's face flushed. "Ha, Brian says that I am always rubbing my belly. I don't even know that I am doing it. No response yet, but I know they can feel it."

"Will you find out if they are a boy or girl?"

"Nope, we just want healthy. Whatever else comes with them, we will be overjoyed."

"Nice. I love that. There are not enough surprises in the world. Why not enjoy the few that you can still get? So, how is Brian doing?"

"Oh, he is great, but overprotective. He won't let me do anything. I remind him that there are women all around the world who work, tend their farms, other children, etcetera while being pregnant. I think I can manage a little food shopping."

"Enjoy it now, because when the baby comes, they say everything changes."

"I think he is being that way because I am considered high risk."

"High risk? Why?"

"Because of my age."

"Yeah, so what? You are only forty-two."

"Yes, I know, but I guess that is considered old to have a baby. I feel amazing and would not have done it any other way."

"I am so happy that everything is working out for you."

After lunch, we did a little baby shopping at a cute boutique. To see Reva waddle around, *oohing* and *ahhing* over onesies and Teddy bears was a beautiful sight to behold.

By the time we got back to the house, Reva was ready to put her feet up. She was retaining water and just needed to relax for a while.

"Reva, this house is amazing. When you said you wanted a yard, I guess you got one."

"Yes, Brian found this place through a friend. There is still some work that needs to be done, but we are in no rush. Everything works, and we need to replenish the bank account before we make any major changes. Hey, do you mind if I lay down for a little while?"

"No, take it easy. I brought a book and will make myself at home."

While Reva took a nap, I found a nice, sunny nook in the kitchen, made myself some tea, and settled in to read. I also called Hendrix, letting him know I had arrived and gave him a rundown of our visit thus far.

"Sounds like pregnancy has been a little difficult on Reva."

"Sort of, but she is handling it fine. There are so many changes going on in her body right now that she just needs to take it easy." I paused. "Do you think forty-two is too old to have a child?"

"Not at all. If the woman is healthy, then it should be fine. Would you like to have a baby?" Hendrix asked shyly.

Whoa, where had that come from? We had never discussed having a baby. I just hadn't thought about it.

I paused to think. "To be perfectly honest, I haven't thought about it. But if it were to happen, I know I would be happy about it."

"Having Aja in my life has opened my eyes to the beauty of fatherhood. If that is a gift that you and I are given, I know you would be a wonderful mother."

"Aw … Thank you, and you would be … What am I saying? You already are an amazing father. Hey, Brian, just got home. I have to jump off. Will call you tonight."

"Okay. Tell them both I said hello and congratulations again."

"Will do. Love you."

"Love you."

I greeted Brian at the door. "Welcome home."

"Hey, Evie. So glad you could come out for a visit. Where is Reva?"

"She wanted to lie down. After our lunch, we did a little shopping. She just needed some rest."

"Good. I am glad that she is listening to her body. I am always telling her to rest."

"What are you two talking about?" Reva interrupted.

"You, sweetheart. We are talking about how you need to rest when your body says so."

Reva walked over and kissed Brian. Then she looked over at me. "See what I mean."

"So, Evie, I know you don't get off island often and you enjoy different types of cuisine. What can I pick up for us to eat tonight?"

"I was going to cook," Reva told him.

"Not tonight, sweetheart. Take it easy and enjoy your time with Evie. So, Evie, what will it be? What are you craving?"

"I'm easy. What about Italian? A nice gnocchi would be wonderful. I can cook Italian, but getting gnocchi just right has always escaped me."

"Good choice. I know the perfect place. Sweetheart, what would you like?"

"A Caesar salad with chicken."

"Is that enough?" I asked.

"Yes, that will be perfect. I am craving romaine lettuce, but I would also like to have Tiramisu for dessert."

"Ooo ... Me, too!"

"All right, ladies, sit back and relax, and I will return in a jiffy."

Reva smiled and blew Brian a kiss.

"Married life looks good on you two."

"Thank you. We are very happy."

"You know what Hendrix asked me today?"

"What?"

"If I wanted to have a baby."

"Really? And, what did you say?"

"That I haven't thought about it, but seeing you and Brian and the joy that you have makes it pretty enticing. I told him, if we were given the gift, I would be happy."

***

An hour later, Brian returned with bags and bags of food. I thought he might have bought out the restaurant. Good thing because Reva was getting hangry.

The food was perfect, and the company even better. We ate and laughed all evening.

"I better be careful hanging out with you two. If I keep on eating like this, people will think that *I'm* pregnant."

"It's just our way of showing you our love," Brian replied.

For the rest of the weekend, we relaxed, told stories, and discussed baby names.

"If it is a girl, I propose we call her Samantha with the nickname of Sammie, and if it is a boy, I like Matthew," Reva said.

Brian scrunched up his nose. "I would prefer Julia for a girl and Coletrain for a boy."

"Hmm … Those are great names. I once met a little girl back in Colorado who opened my eyes to seeing things in a different way. Her name was Sammy, so if I had to choose from what you both said, I would say Samantha for a girl and Coletrain for a boy. How are you going to decide?"

"Well, we have a few more months to go, and I can be pretty persuasive," Reva said with a smile.

The weekend flew by, and Monday morning, my bag was packed and I was ready to head back to island life. Reva and I said our goodbyes, and then Brian brought me to the bus station.

"Are you sure everything is okay with Reva? Her morning sickness isn't letting up."

"She has weekly appointments with her doctor, and she says this is not unusual."

"Keep me posted on how things go. As you have learned, Reva can be stubborn. If you need help, just let me know."

"Thanks, Evie. I will keep that in my back pocket. If she won't rest, I will threaten to call you. I am sure she will oblige."

The bus ride home gave me lots of time to think about what Hendrix had asked. Could we start a family? Was I too old? I put my hand on my belly and closed my eyes. Then I thought about how wonderful it would be for Granddad to see his great-grandchild.

Higher self, I am open and allowing to whatever the Universe has in store for us.

As I stared out the window, watching the world go by, I felt at peace.

CHAPTER 16 — ALWAYS WITH YOU

Tonight, Granddad was coming over for dinner and a movie. Interestingly, he had asked that we have lobster and chowder. For some reason, though, he wanted me to make the chowder.

"You trust me making your chowder?"

"I taught you, right?"

"Yes, but I have never done it before. Will you watch to make sure that I don't make a mistake?"

"Sure. The hogs are fresh, so you can't mess it up."

He shucked, and I ground them up. I made the rouge, added the vegetables, potatoes, hogs, seasoning, and milk. Then I let it cook.

"Stop looking in the pot. It's not going anywhere."

"I just want to make sure it looks good."

"Trust yourself, Evie. You know how to cook. I know it will be amazing."

We steamed the lobsters, and then Granddad grabbed a couple of beers from the refrigerator as we sat down to our feast.

"Looks and smells great, Evie."

"This is a hell of a dinner for midweek. Are we celebrating something?"

"Nope. Just wanted to make sure you knew what you were doing before I headed out."

"Headed out? Where are you going?"

"You know, Evie, I will not be around forever."

"Granddad, I just made this wonderful dinner; let's not have that kind of talk now. You aren't going anywhere. Remember, not old, just wiser."

After dinner, we enjoyed a good ole Sci-Fi movie then called it a night.

Granddad gave me a hug and said, "Thanks for dinner, kid. You did good."

"Thanks, Granddad. I love you. See you tomorrow."

"Not if I see you first."

***

Making Granddad's chowder had been an amazing accomplishment. It was like I had earned my stripes. For the next week, all I heard from Granddad was how good that chowder had turned out. Even Barbra, from over at the library, said that she had heard I had learned how to make it. To surprise Granddad, I made him another pot, but this time I even dug the quahogs myself. However, when I slipped through the bushes to deliver it, I felt something was off.

Granddad did not greet me.

I knocked, but there was no answer. His truck was still in the driveway, so I opened the door slowly and could hear labored breathing. I rushed down the hall to Granddad's room. He was lying in bed, still in his sleep clothes from the night before. His face was pale.

"Granddad, what's wrong?"

In a soft but heavy voice, he said, "Evie, I am tired."

"Did you take your medicine?"

"No, kid."

"What? Where is it? Let me call the hospital."

"No, Evie, no more."

I dropped to my knees at his bedside and took his hand. "Please, no, Granddad. Don't leave me. Please, don't. I can't do this without you."

"Evie, I have given you everything that I could in this physical world. The secrets that were kept from you have all been shared, and you have been told why we did what we did. Through the eyes of love, you took control. It opened your heart and allowed you to feel. You are a strong, indigenous woman, and I am very proud to be your granddad. My time here is done. I have stayed long enough, and it is time for me to go home. Your grandmother and father have been waiting for me.

"I love you, my dear. Live your life to the fullest and enjoy this journey. Share your love and light with this world. Fly, my little bird ... fly." With that, Granddad took one final breath then slowly closed his eyes.

I buckled over, unable to catch my breath. It was like someone had just punched me in the gut. All my wind was gone. Slowly, the tears fell. Then I wiped my eyes, caught my breath, and raised my head. Looking at Granddad's peaceful face, I caressed his cheek, laid my head on his smooth, weathered hand, and sobbed.

***

The spirit fire was lit and maintained until the funeral. It seemed like the entire island had known Granddad, and people were coming from everywhere to give their condolences. Hendrix, Reva, and Brian had all flown in for the service, but Steve was my emotional rock. He was the first person who I had called to tell the news, and he stayed with me through the entire process. I knew there was a part of him that felt like he had lost a family member, as well.

For the next couple of months, I couldn't do anything. No painting, limited phone calls, and no visitors. I felt lost.

Hendrix would check in on me daily, either by call or text, but the conversations were short. Steve and Celeste would sneak in and leave me food to make sure I ate. Steve and Beth took over the Something-Something Painting Program in my absence. Luckily, the principal understood.

Then, one morning, I heard a truck coming up the road. I went to the door to see who it was. Not recognizing the truck, I walked outside.

"Evie?"

"Yes."

"Hi, you may not remember me, but it's Louie. We met at the tribal offices a while ago."

"Yes, yes, I remember you. Hi. How can I help you?"

"It's time."

"Time for what?"

"To set yourself free."

"I'm sorry, I don't understand."

"Before your granddad passed, he asked that, when the time was right, I take you out on the water so that you could release his ashes. Last night, in my dreams, he came to me and said it was time. It's time to set you free."

"What do you mean, set *me* free?"

"Evie, he is still here with us—with you. He knew you would feel an obligation to stay on the island. That is not what he wanted. He was so proud of you and that you wanted to see new places and have new experiences. Attaquin never wanted to hold you back during his life, and especially not now in death. He wants you to embrace your free spirit and truly live your life, to be free to do what you choose."

Tears stained my cheeks, and the lump in my throat kept me from saying a word. Grief overtook me. My body shook, shoulders slumped, and my weeping became increasingly louder. Louie came over and wrapped me in a loving hug.

"I miss him so much. I don't want to let him go," I sobbed out.

"He is not gone; only his physical body left this world. He is here with you now. Close your eyes and breathe. Take a deep breath and clear your mind. Feel his energy all around you."

At that moment, I could feel goosebumps run up and down my arms, and I felt a wonderful tingling sensation on the top of my head. Feeling that energy brought a smile to my face. I knew Louie was right; I knew Granddad was with me. But through my grief, I had become closed off and could not feel him.

I went into the house, grabbed a jacket and Granddad's urn, and then Louie helped me into his truck. We drove to the beach in silence. This would be the first time since Granddad's passing that I had been down to the water.

When we got there, we climbed into the dinghy, and Louie paddled us out to Granddad's boat. The keys were right where they always were—in the side compartment. Granddad never locked his boat. Everyone knew it was his, and he believed, if someone stole it, then they needed it more than he did.

Louie took us out slowly through the channel. Then, once we were clear, he opened her up. The water was calm, and the ride was exhilarating.

Just at the tip of the island, right in front of the lighthouse, Louie stopped the boat. The waves slapping against the hull was the only thing I could hear.

"This is the place, Evie."

I looked at Louie then walked to the front of the boat. I stood there, taking in the beauty of everything around me—the ocean, the lighthouse, and the clay cliffs. So strong and peaceful, just like Granddad.

Slowly, I opened the urn and let the soft breeze spread his ashes over the one place that he loved to be the most—the ocean.

Before closing the urn, I whispered, "Thank you, Granddad, for always being there for me, for teaching me, and helping me become the person I am today. I love you." I took a deep breath and looked up to the sky. At that moment, a hawk flew overhead, and I heard Granddad whisper in my ear, *"Fly, my little bird, fly."*

***

I woke early and went out on the deck. I missed hearing Granddad putzing around outside. Today, however, instead of crying about it, the thought brought a slight smile to my face. As each new day passed, I felt a peace growing within me. Today, I would get out and start living my life again.

As that thought crossed my mind, I heard a hawk's cry. Under my breath, I said, "Good morning, Granddad."

My desire to get out brought me to the lighthouse. It was quiet, so I took the opportunity to meditate against her. Her coolness and strength ran throughout my body.

I slipped easily into meditation and was greeted by my mother. Her warmth surrounded me like a loving hug. Quietly, I heard. *"Evie, it is your turn. Take the leap."*

I opened my eyes and knew exactly what to do. I took one deep breath and declared, "It's time."

THE END

REFERENCES

Crystal Vaults. "Emerald Meaning and Uses." Retrieved November 7, 2021 at https://www.crystalvaults.com/crystal-encyclopedia/emerald.

Fondin, Michelle. "The Root Chakra. Muladhara." Retrieved December 13, 2021 at https://chopra.com/articles/the-root-chakra-muladhara.

Wallis, Brad. "How Your Soul Experiences Taste." Retrieved December 13, 2021 at www.gaia.com/article/how-your-soul-experiences-taste.

Putri, Edira. *Culture Trip*. "Traditional Balinese Dishes You Need to Try." Retrieved February 6, 2022 at https://theculturetrip.com/asia/Indonesia/article/10-traditional-balinese-dishes-you-need-to-try.

Hoot. "6 Must-Try Sweet Treats (Desserts & Cakes) in Bali." Retrieved February 6, 2022 at https://www.hootholidays.com.au/blog/bali/6-must-try-sweet-treats-in-bali.

Sorrentino, Lori. *Travlinmad Slow Travel Blog*. "Breakfast in Bali: A Mouth-Watering Expression of Local Culture." Retrieved February 6, 2022 at https://www.travlinmad.com/ blog/breakfast-in-bali.

White, Annette. *Bucket List Journey*. "Bali Points of Interest: 1-Day Itinerary in Indonesia's Popular Cruise Port."

Retrieved February 6, 2022 at https://bucketlistjourney.net/bali-points-of-interest.

Read the entire *Evie Prince* Series

ABOUT THE AUTHOR

Inspirational writer, Victoria Wright, has embarked on a journey to find her true self. In the process, she is remembering how to be whole, to look inward for guidance, and to know her truth. Her journey is full of beauty and discovery. She invites you to embark on your own journey of remembering.

Victoria is from Martha's Vineyard, Massachusetts, and she is a member of the Wampanoag Tribe of Gay Head Aquinnah. Currently, she and her family reside just outside of Denver, Colorado.

www.ingramcontent.com/pod-product-compliance
Lightning Source LLC
Chambersburg PA
CBHW030907080526
44589CB00010B/189